The Great Depression

The Great Depression

An International Disaster of Perverse Economic Policies

THOMAS E. HALL

and

J. DAVID FERGUSON

Ann Arbor

THE UNIVERSITY OF MICHIGAN PRESS

Copyright © by the University of Michigan 1998
All rights reserved
Published in the United States of America by
The University of Michigan Press
Manufactured in the United States of America
⊚ Printed on acid-free paper

2001   2000   1999   1998   4   3   2   1

A CIP catalog record for this book is available from the British Library.

Library of Congress Cataloging-in-Publication Data

Hall, Thomas E. (Thomas Emerson), 1954–
    The Great Depression : an international disaster of perverse
economic policies / Thomas E. Hall and J. David Ferguson.
       p.   cm.
    Includes bibliographical references and index.
    ISBN 0-472-09667-2 (acid-free). — ISBN 0-472-06667-6 (pbk. : acid-free)
    1. Depressions—1929—United States.   2. Depressions—1929—
Europe.   3. Europe—Economic conditions—1918–1945.   4. United
States—Economic conditions—1918–1945.   5. International economic
relations.   I. Ferguson, J. David, 1940–   .   II. Title.
HB3717 1929 .H325   1998
338.5'42—dc21   97-21196
                                                                       CIP

To Christine and Alexander
T.E.H.

To Kathy
J.D.F.

Contents

Preface

The Great Depression must be on any list of the top ten most important events of the twentieth century. It featured the worst economic recession the United States, and several other countries as well, ever experienced. The resulting pain and misery ravaged huge segments of several countries' populations, so extensively that enormous social upheaval occurred in countries that experienced the worst economic devastation. The two major countries that were hit the hardest were the United States and Germany, and not surprisingly these are the two countries that experienced the greatest political and social changes. The United States ended up with the New Deal and the legacy of a greatly expanded federal government. Germany ended up with Adolf Hitler and National Socialism.

The Depression occurred more than six decades ago. As the years have passed society's collective memory has naturally faded. After all, anyone who was a young adult in their early twenties when the Depression began would now be nearly ninety years old. Sadly, the number of people who endured it is diminishing rapidly.

While neither of us lived through the Depression, our parents and grandparents did. We grew up hearing firsthand stories from our relatives about their experiences. Some of them witnessed and took part in bank runs, some were laid off from work, and one received his final pay in the form of office furniture because his employer had run out of money. At least one relative lost a significant amount of wealth in the stock market crash. Certain of our family members had to leave the city and move back onto the family farm because there they could help with the work and earn food for their immediate families. Some of our relatives were employed by the federal government in New Deal programs—in fact one worked on building the Hoover Dam. These stories left an indelible mark on us because we personally have never had to experience the kind of hardships that our parents and grandparents did during the Great Depression.

A young person today is a generation or two further removed from the Depression than we are and so is much less likely to have heard such stories. In fact, today's young people seem to have a rather weak sense of just what the Great Depression was and why it was so important. This is hardly surprising because they didn't grow up listening to firsthand stories, the kind of dramatic history that captures your attention and changes your thinking. Yet at the same time it is important that they know what happened and why it happened.

We wrote this book largely for two reasons. One is that over the years we have watched macroeconomics as it is taught at the college level become increasingly theoretical and (in our opinion) less interesting. Macroeconomics is most enjoyable when it can be applied to actual events, and what better to apply it to than the greatest macroeconomic disaster in U.S. history? The Depression provides a fascinating blend of economic history, monetary and fiscal policy, international finance, money and banking, and aggregate supply and demand anaiysis. Studying the 1930s helps bring macroeconomics to life.

The second reason we wrote this book is because there is a story we wanted to tell. It is the tale of powerful, well-intentioned people in several countries who committed an incredible sequence of policy errors that generated a cataclysmic event reaching around the entire globe. The disasters of the 1930s were not caused by some uncontrollable event such as the eruption of Mt. Vesuvius that buried Pompeii. Instead the Depression was caused by people with good intentions carrying out misguided economic policies that they thought were proper, but that actually created an absolute disaster. We would think that this economic calamity would be punishment enough for one generation, but the Depression ultimately led to World War II in Europe and the deaths of tens of millions of people. There's a saying: "The road to hell is paved with good intentions." It's hard to find a period in history where that phrase better applies.

We owe debts of gratitude to a number of people for their efforts in helping bring this project to completion. Our wives, Christine Hall and Katherine Ferguson, read some of the chapters in draft form and provided comments. In addition, they provided ongoing moral support. Two anonymous reviewers provided very helpful comments. Two of our graduate assistants, Brett Hendrickson and Masahiro Kawai, helped with data analysis, proofreading, and checking bibliographic references. Finally, Christopher Ferguson provided extremely helpful technical assistance. Any remaining errors are our responsibility.

Great Depression Timeline

1914 World War I breaks out in Europe. European combatants abandon the gold standard.

1917 United States enters World War I.

1918 World War I ends.

1919 Treaty of Versailles signed; Allied embargo against Germany lifted.

1923 German hyperinflation.

1924 German hyperinflation ends. Dawes Plan that reduces Germany's reparations payments takes effect; U.S. lending to Germany begins; Germany returns to the gold standard.

1925 United Kingdom returns to gold standard at $4.86/pound, the same parity ratio that existed when World War I erupted. At this rate, the pound is overvalued, which places Britain in a balance-of-payments deficit that results in a gold outflow from that country. British economic growth slows.

1926 British economic problems worsen. A major labor dispute over wages erupts in the coal industry, and the miners are locked out for seven months. A nationwide general strike lasts nine days.

1927 Central bankers of United States, Britain, France, and Germany hold a meeting on Long Island, New York. Federal Reserve agrees to expand monetary growth to make up for having sterilized the gold inflow from Britain. The monetary expansion sets off U.S. stock market advance and causes U.S. lending to Germany to dry up.

1928 Alarmed by the stock market advance and member banks' loans to brokers, the Federal Reserve begins a series of steps to tighten credit conditions. The U.S. monetary growth rate slows, and U.S. interest rates rise. Foreign central banks raise their interest rates to protect their gold stocks. In November, Hoover wins 1928 presidential election.

1929   Hoover takes office in March. By spring, major growth slowdowns occur in many countries around the world. Most countries are experiencing recessions by summer. U.S. stock market crashes in October, after which the U.S. recession worsens.

1930   Industrialized countries' output continues to drop. First wave of bank failures in the United States occurs in November and December. Smoot-Hawley Tariff Act becomes law.

1931   Second wave of bank failures in the United States begins in March and continues through the rest of the year. In May, a run develops on Austria's largest bank, the KreditAnstalt. The bank runs spread to Germany; their recession deepens. During the summer, a large-scale capital flight from Britain develops that ultimately results in that country abandoning the gold standard and allowing the pound to depreciate. Fear of further devaluations leads to runs on the Japanese yen and U.S. dollar. Japan responds by abandoning the gold standard and pursuing expansionary policies. Recovery soon begins in that country. The United States responds by staying on the gold standard and raising interest rates to protect the gold stock. As a result, the U.S. recession deepens even further.

1932   Germany abandons the gold standard. Expansionary policies set off economic recoveries in Britain and Germany. German reparations payments canceled at the Lausanne Conference. In the United States, Hoover sponsors income tax hike that is passed by Congress. The Federal Reserve begins open market purchase program in response to the threat of congressional actions, and the U.S. economy begins to show signs of recovery. However, the open market purchase program is abandoned during the summer when Congress recesses, and the economic recovery is aborted. The third and final wave of bank runs begins in November. Roosevelt also wins the 1932 presidential election in that month.

1933   Bank runs continue in the United States, and the system finally collapses in February when several states are without a single operating bank. U.S. economy bottoms out in March. Roosevelt takes office in early March and declares a National Bank Holiday; solvent banks reopen a few weeks later, and the economic recovery begins. Major components of the first New Deal legislation are passed by June, which includes U.S. abandonment of the traditional gold standard. In Germany, Adolf Hitler takes office in January, becoming dictator in March.

1934   U.S. economy growing, but at uneven rates. Public dissatisfaction over the New Deal, especially the National Industrial Recovery Act, is growing.

1935   NRA and AAA declared unconstitutional. Roosevelt launches second New Deal that includes National Labor Relations Act (Wagner Act).

1936   U.S. economic recovery strengthens amid widespread labor unrest as firms expect the Wagner Act will be declared unconstitutional. Inflation rate accelerates amid enormous buildup of excess reserves in the U.S. banking system. In response, Federal Reserve begins series of hikes in the required reserve ratio.

1937   As a result of the monetary contraction, U.S. economy plunges into another recession. Public anger over the New Deal intensifies. The Wagner Act is upheld by the Supreme Court. Social Security withholding taxes begin. In Germany, economy reaches full employment.

1938   Federal Reserve initiates monetary expansion in response to rising unemployment. U.S. economy begins to recover.

1939   U.S. monetary expansion continues. Germany and the Soviet Union partition Poland. France and Britain declare war on Germany.

1940   Germany invades France and is victorious six weeks later. The British army withdraws from France at Dunkirk and prepares to carry on the war against Germany from the home island. The United Kingdom begins large-scale orders for war material from United States; in addition, the United States begins its own military buildup. The U.S. economic expansion accelerates.

1941   U.S. economy expanding rapidly, unemployment falling dramatically as the U.S. military buildup continues. In June, World War II spreads when Germany invades the Soviet Union. In December, Japan attacks the U.S. naval base at Pearl Harbor, which causes the United States to become a full-fledged combatant in World War II. The U.S. economy is close to full employment by the end of the year. The Depression is over.

CHAPTER 1

What Happened?

———⇒‑◇‑⇐———

*One vivid, gruesome moment of those dark days we shall never
forget. We saw a crowd of some fifty men fighting over a barrel
of garbage which had been set outside the back door of a restau-
rant. American citizens fighting for scraps of food like animals!*
—*Louise Armstrong, describing an incident
she witnessed in Chicago during the
spring of 1932 (1938, 10)*

———⇒‑◇‑⇐———

The Great Depression in the United States occurred from 1929 to 1941.
The worst of it was during the first three and a half years when virtually
every single indicator of economic prosperity reflected the disaster. The
falling levels of economic output resulted in widespread human misery,
the extent of which is measured by the rising level of unemployment,
increased poverty, and high rates of default on debt by both firms and
households. The Depression was so severe that the human perspective
and drama of the events cannot truly be shown through these numbers.
It led to huge changes in our social fabric. Large migrations of people
occurred from the dust bowl areas of mid-America to more prosperous
places like California, and from the rural south to the industrial north.
There were food riots, violent labor strikes, and widespread discontent
that made many fearful that the socialist or communist political parties
might enjoy great gains in popularity or even rise to power. Some might
say that such a revolution indeed happened—through Franklin D. Roosevelt and the New Deal.

—————⊰•⊱—————

Only when things went economically wrong for [Germany] . . . did the Nazi Party flourish and vice versa. Their election successes and membership rose and fell in exact parallel to the unemployment figures. During the years of prosperity between 1924 and 1928 the Nazis as good as disappeared from the political arena. But . . . the deeper the [economy] . . . subsided into crisis, the more firmly did the fascist party sit in the saddle.
—*Alfred Sohn-Rethel (1978, 133)*

—————⊰•⊱—————

The Depression was not confined to just the United States. Virtually every major industrialized country experienced it to varying degrees. In fact, it is this aspect of the Depression that is most tragic. Without the Depression in Germany, it is highly unlikely that Adolf Hitler and the National Socialists would have risen to power. But they did gain power and went on to unleash terrible forces in Europe that led to the deaths of tens of millions of people, horrible destruction, and pain and suffering beyond anything we could imagine. A very strong case can be made that if the Great Depression had not occurred, World War II in Europe would not have either.[1] Given the terrible violence and human misery associated with the Great Depression, perhaps the saddest thing is that the whole affair could have been avoided. The Depression was the result of human errors in the area of economic policy. As you will learn from reading this book, a great many mistakes were made by well-meaning people in both business and government who were grossly ignorant about the goals, tools, and impact of economic policy.

In terms of macroeconomics, the Great Depression is important for three reasons. First, it was the impetus for John Maynard Keynes to write his magnum opus *The General Theory of Employment, Interest, and Money* (1936). This book represents Keynes's attempt to explain the causes of the widespread unemployment around the world. In this book Keynes develops his quasi-general equilibrium analysis that marks the birth of modern macroeconomics.[2] With this development, the field of macroeconomics made a great leap forward.

Second, since the Great Depression includes the single most severe recession the United States has ever experienced, macroeconomists are naturally interested in understanding and explaining its causes. In fact, Bernanke says that "to understand the Great Depression is the Holy Grail of macroeconomics" (1995, 1). Given the debates in macroeconomics about which model best explains economic activity, an explanation of the Great Depression is considered an important test for any macroeconomic model.

Finally, the Great Depression led to an enormous expansion in the size of the U.S. federal government. With the large declines in economic output associated with the Depression, the public demanded help, and the federal government responded by enacting a wide variety of programs under the guise of the New Deal. With the enactment of these programs the federal government became a much more important player in the national economy than it had been before. In 1929 federal purchases of goods and services accounted for only 1.3 percent of gross domestic product (GDP). By 1939 it accounted for 7.1 percent of GDP. In addition, the federal government entered a wide variety of areas it had not previously been involved in, such as securities regulation, welfare, social security, collecting unemployment data, and electric generation and transmission to name just a few. The growth and size of the federal government that so many people complain about today has its roots in the 1930s.

Perhaps the worst thing about this Depression was its inexorable continuance year after year. Men who have been sturdy and self-respecting workers can take unemployment without flinching for a few weeks, a few months, even if they have to see their families suffer; but it is different after a year . . . two years . . . three years . . .
—*Frederick Lewis Allen (1940, 49)*

In the United States the Great Depression consisted of two major recessions that kept economic output, measured as real GDP, below estimated full employment output for 12 years. This pattern is shown in figure 1.1 where real GDP and Gordon's (1993) full employment measure are plotted for the period 1919 through 1941. The 1920s are included in this figure and the following ones to provide a contrast between the relatively stable 1920s and the highly unstable 1930s. During the 1920s the U.S. economy experienced vibrant growth; in fact the average annual growth rate during the decade was almost twice the long-run average over the past century. But that growth was followed by the first recession (1929–33) of the Great Depression. This recession was termed the "Great Contraction" by Friedman and Schwartz (1963), and it was by far the worst of the two. In fact, it is the worst economic downturn in U.S. history since 1848 when records begin. From August 1929 to March 1933 real GDP fell by about 25 percent, and nominal GDP by about 50 percent. At the trough in March 1933 the unemployment rate peaked at 24.9 percent of the labor force.[3] The ensuing expansion from 1933 to 1937 was fairly strong, but not enough to drive output back up to anywhere near the full employment level. That recovery was aborted by the second recession that began in 1937; output fell again, and the Great Depression was considerably prolonged in the United States. It took three years of economic recovery, from 1938 through 1941, for output to approach its full employment level.

> Unless some counteracting clause comes along to prevent the fall in the price level, such a depression as that of 1929–33 . . . tends to continue, going deeper, in a vicious spiral, for many years. There is then no tendency of the boat to stop tipping until it has capsized.
>
> —*Irving Fisher (1933, 346)*

The price level (measured as the GDP deflator) is plotted in figure 1.2. The striking feature about this series is that the high degree of price stability from 1921 to 1929 was followed by a major deflation during the Great Contraction of 1929 to 1933. During this recession the price level, measured as the GDP deflator, fell by about 25 percent. Once the expansion began in 1933 the price level reversed course and rose until the second recession began in 1937. This pattern is interesting: inflation accelerated from 1933 to 1936 despite huge excess capacity suggested by the double-digit unemployment rates that prevailed at the time. This is unusual behavior; normally the inflation rate falls when excess capacity exists.

> The effects of the banking crisis on interest rates show up clearly in the renewed and far more drastic rise in yields on lower grade corporate bonds, as banks sought to realize on their portfolios and in the process forced bond prices ever lower. By that time, too, the economic contraction had seriously impaired the earn-

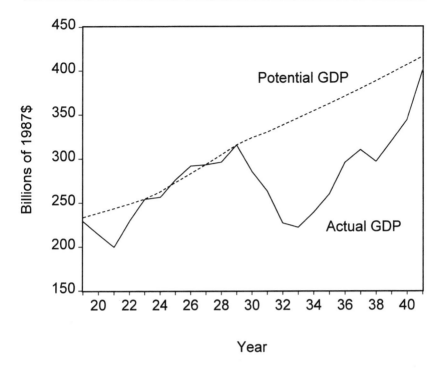

Fig. 1.1. Actual and potential GDP

ing power of many concerns and sharply raised the chances of default.

> —*Milton Friedman and Anna J. Schwartz (1963, 315)*

The behavior of interest rates is shown in figure 1.3 where the short-term commercial paper rate and the long-term corporate bond rate are plotted. The corporate bond rate is on Baa rated bonds which are the lower-grade bonds that Friedman and Schwartz refer to above. Notable here are the rising short-term rates during the late 1920s followed by the very low short-term rates during the mid- and late 1930s. Another interesting feature is the slow downward trend in corporate bond rates during the 1920s followed by the major rise during the early 1930s. At one point (mid-1932) they surpassed 10 percent. When considered along with the major deflation going on at the time, ex post real interest rates were extremely high, in the neighborhood of around 15 percent.[4]

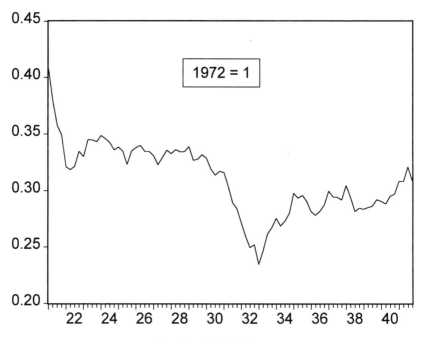

Fig. I.2.   GNP deflator

The singular feature of the great crash of 1929 was that the worst continued to worsen. What looked one day like the end proved on the next day to have been only the beginning. Nothing could have been more ingeniously designed to maximize the suffering, and also to insure that as few as possible escaped the common misfortune. . . . The Coolidge bull market was a remarkable phenomenon. The ruthlessness of its liquidation was, in its own way, equally remarkable.
                                    —*John Kenneth Galbraith (1954, 108–9).*

An index of common stock prices is plotted in figure 1.4. Stock prices rose rapidly during the late 1920s with gains of 25 percent during 1927, 38 percent during 1928, and 30 percent during the first eight months of 1929. These gains were, of course, followed by the crash in October 1929, but the crash was hardly the end of the story as stock prices con-

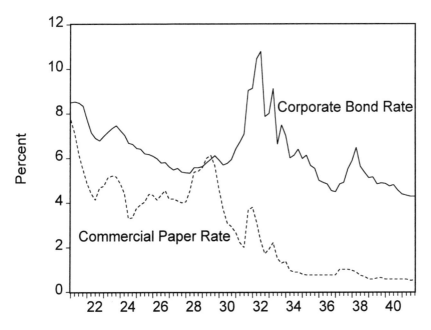

Fig. I.3.   Commercial paper and corporate bond rates

tinued to plummet before bottoming out in 1932. The total decline in the index from 1929 to 1932 was 82 percent. Stock prices did not reattain their 1929 level until 1954.

For if effective demand is deficient, not only is the public scandal of wasted resources intolerable, but the individual enterpriser who seeks to bring these resources into action is operating with the odds loaded against him. . . . But if effective demand is adequate, average skill and average good fortune will be enough.
—*John Maynard Keynes (1936, 381)*

Keynes is certainly the dominant economic policy figure to be heard from during the 1930s. As mentioned earlier, he wrote *The General Theory* to explain the Depression. In a nutshell, Keynes thought the Depression was the result of a lack of effective demand. Using today's terminology we would call it a low level of aggregate demand. His

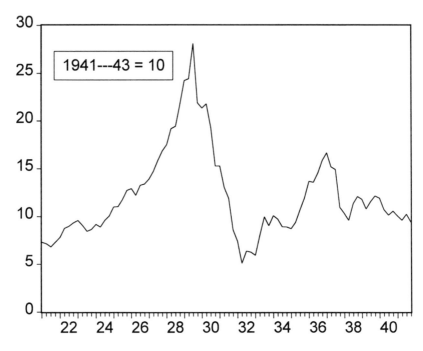

Fig. 1.4.   Index of common stock prices

income-expenditure approach to aggregate demand describes aggregate demand as the sum of spending on consumption goods and services, investment goods, government purchases, and net exports. Figures 1.5 through 1.8 plot these spending components in constant dollar (that is, real) values. These diagrams clearly illustrate the major booms in both consumption and investment spending followed by across-the-board declines from 1929 through 1933. Perhaps most notable is the absolute collapse of investment spending shown in figure 1.6. During 1932, reduction of inventories by business (that is, disinvestment) was large enough to offset the other components of investment spending to make total gross investment negative.

Another interesting data series is government purchases (fig. 1.7). The series is procyclical, which means moving in the same direction as GDP and the business cycle. In other words, governments cut spending in the face of falling production and rising unemployment. Also note the

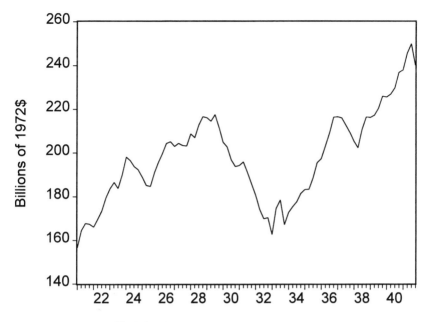

Fig. 1.5 .   Real consumption expenditures

huge bulge in spending in 1940 and 1941, the result of the U.S. military buildup following Germany's defeat of France.

⟹⟐⟸

It is hardly conceivable that money income could have declined by over one-half and prices by over one-third in the course of four years if there had been no decline in the stock of money.
—*Milton Friedman and Anna J. Schwartz (1963, 301)*

⟹⟐⟸

Figure 1.9 shows the stock of money measured as M2. The series grew steadily during the 1920s, but following its peak in 1929 it plummeted through to 1933. The spending decline of 1929 through 1933 was clearly associated with the falling stock of money. To identify the source of the decline in the money stock, it is useful to consider an equation that characterizes the factors determining the stock of money:

$$M = [(1 + cd)/(cd + rd)] \, B$$

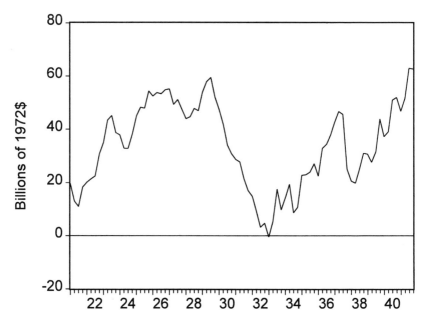

Fig. 1.6.   Real investment expenditures

where M is the stock of money, cd is the currency–deposit ratio (currency in the hands of the public divided by total bank deposits), rd is the reserve–deposit ratio (bank reserves divided by bank deposits), and B is the monetary base (bank reserves plus currency in the hands of the public). The term $[(1 + cd)/(cd + rd)]$ is called the money multiplier.

The monetary base and money multiplier are plotted in figure 1.10. While base growth was slow during the late 1920s and early 1930s, this is clearly not the reason why the stock of money declined by the amount that it did. The money multiplier was the culprit, and it fell by about 50 percent from 1929 to 1933. So while the monetary base rose 17 percent, the stock of money fell by about 33 percent. The source of the decline in the money multiplier is shown in figure 1.11 where we can see both the reserve–deposit ratio (rd) and currency–deposit ratio (cd).[5] After years of relative stability during the 1920s both measures rose significantly during the early 1930s. This drove down the money multiplier and is the reason why the stock of money fell so dramatically. We can also see that the currency–deposit ratio reversed direction after 1933 with the stabilization of

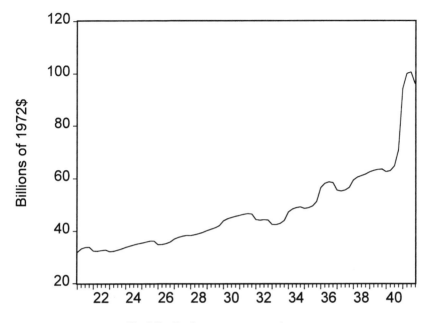

Fig. 1.7.   Real government purchases

the banking system and the advent of deposit insurance. The reserve–deposit ratio continued its upward climb until 1939.

A final point to raise about monetary behavior during the 1930s is the rapid monetary growth during the late 1930s. Referring back to figure 1.9, from 1938 to 1941 the stock of money rose rapidly, but the recovery was weak until 1940–41. This behavior turned out to be important because many economists interpreted it to mean that monetary policy had a weak effect on output.

This brief look at the behavior of some key economic variables during the 1930s presents us with a set of questions we must answer if we are to understand what happened during the 1930s and why it happened.

1. Did factors building up during the 1920s set the stage for the Great Depression? The 1920s were an era of great prosperity, especially for urban Americans. Did the Great Depression amount to "payback time"? Was the Great Depression a natural correction following the prosperous twenties?

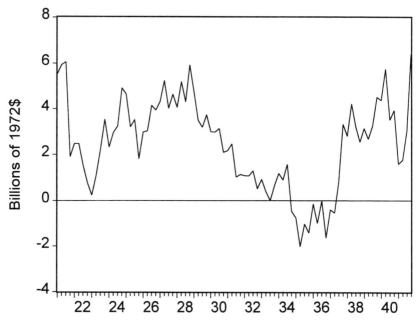

Fig. I.8.   Real net exports

2. Why was the Depression so severe? What happened to make the 1929–33 recession the worst on record?

3. Why did the Depression last so long in the United States? Output was below the estimated full-employment level for twelve years. Germany's economy was back to full employment by 1937, four years ahead of the United States. Why didn't the U.S. economy return to full employment sooner?

4. Why was it worldwide? Every major industrialized country in the world, and several other less developed countries as well, experienced recessions during the late 1920s and early 1930s. While they varied in duration and depth of falling production and employment, in most cases they were fairly severe, especially in the United States, Germany, and Canada. Industrial production fell by about 50 percent in each of these countries.

5. Why wasn't the U.S. economy able to grow during the mid-1930s without a significant acceleration of the inflation rate? Despite

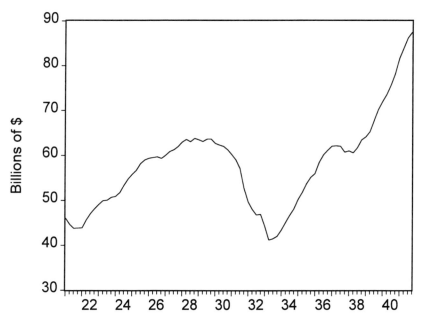

Fig. 1.9.   Money stock, M2

extremely high labor force unemployment rates, the fact is that the U.S. economy experienced an acceleration of inflation during the mid-1930s. This rise in inflation was large enough to persuade the Federal Reserve that steps needed to be taken to slow credit expansion. These policy moves helped generate the 1937–38 recession.

6. Why did the reserve–deposit and currency–deposit ratios rise so dramatically and result in the major decline in the stock of money? Given our look here at the economic series, an obvious part of the story about the Great Depression is the behavior of the stock of money. We have seen the pattern of the reserve–deposit and currency–deposit ratios; what caused these variables to become so unstable?

7. What caused the Depression to end? A weak economy during the mid- and late 1930s showed little sign of getting out of the Depression. But then the economy rebounded sharply in 1940–41. What were the factors that caused this to happen?

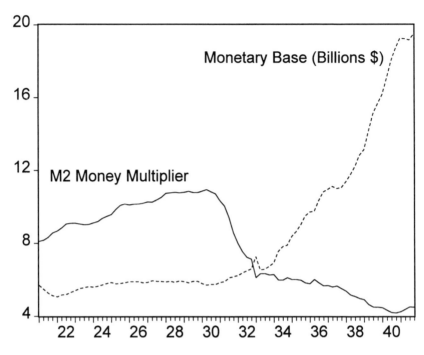

Fig. 1.10.   Monetary base and M2 multiplier

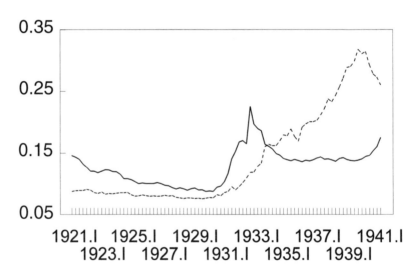

Fig. 1.11.   C/D and R/D ratios (solid line = C/D ratio; dashed line = R/D ratio)

Our purpose here is to answer these questions in an attempt to provide a thorough analysis of the Great Depression. To accomplish this task, we draw upon the abundance of existing literature on the subject. We begin our investigation by studying the U.S. economy during the 1920s. Did a major recession necessarily have to follow the vibrant growth of the 1920s?

CHAPTER 2

Payback Time?

—=»-0-«=—

As you look at the high prices recorded on September 3, 1929, remember that on that day few people imagined that the peak had actually been reached. The enormous majority fully expected the Big Bull Market to go on and on.

—*Frederick Lewis Allen (1931, 226)*

The collapse in the stock market in the autumn of 1929 was implicit in the speculation that went before.

—*John Kenneth Galbraith (1954, 169)*

—=»-0-«=—

2.1. They Were the Good Old Days

The 1920s were a period of significant prosperity in the United States. From the end of the recession in July 1921 to the economic peak in August 1929 that preceded the Great Depression, economic output growth averaged 5.9 percent per year, and that figure includes output declines during two mild recessions that occurred in 1923–24 and 1926–27. This economic growth is quite remarkable when one considers that the long-run average growth rate of the U.S. economy is around 3.0 percent per year.

This vibrant growth was associated with rapid improvements in living standards for urban Americans. This was the time when many middle-class Americans obtained automobiles, electrical appliances, and their own houses. Potter notes that during the 1920s the number of residences rose 25 percent, telephones increased 54 percent, food production went up about 50 percent, the number of automobiles registered went from 9 million in 1920 to 23 million in 1929, kilowatt-hours of electricity generated more than doubled, and there were enormous increases in sales of electrical cooking devices, vacuums, and radios (1974). At the same time, consumption of education and recreational services boomed as well. Potter contends that the decade "amounted to a massive increase in consumption, perhaps greater in total and *per capita* than in any previous decade in American history" (1974, 48).

The output gains of the 1920s were associated with mild deflation as the GNP deflator fell at an average annual rate of 0.5 percent from 1921 to 1929. In other words, the aggregate supply schedule was shifting to the right more rapidly than the aggregate demand schedule was. The major source of the rapid growth of aggregate supply was widespread application of assembly-line techniques in several industries including household appliances, food processing, and tobacco. The resulting productivity gains were such that while total employment in manufacturing was roughly constant from 1920 to 1929, output grew over 60 percent.

The increased ownership and use of autos was an important stimulus to growth. In fact, it is difficult to overstate the role of the automobile in helping to generate the economic gains of the 1920s. Thanks to the cost reductions resulting from the application of modern mass production techniques by Ford Motor Company in 1913, retail prices for the Model T fell from $950 per auto in 1908 to $290 by 1924 (Williamson 1951, 728). At such prices a Model T (and many other competing models) became affordable for middle-class families. As a result, auto ownership rose significantly during the 1910s and through the 1920s. At the same time, many roads were being paved, which stimulated the use of the autos. From 1920 through 1929 the number of miles of surface roads nearly doubled from 388,000 to 626,000 (Potter 1974, 47). The resulting increase in both the number of automobiles and their use generated a massive stimulus to the demand for complementary goods and services. The petroleum industry boomed, as did the production of tires, traffic signals, service stations, and everything else associated with auto use at that time. Experience gained in these growing industries likely resulted in more efficient production techniques and improving productivity.[1]

While technology-based productivity gains were stimulating aggregate supply, aggregate demand grew as well. The sources of aggregate demand growth according to the income-expenditure approach are shown in table 2.1. Clearly, the bulk of demand growth during the decade is accounted for by spending on consumption goods and services. The role of consumer durables during the decade is illustrated by the fact that from 1921 to 1929 consumption spending on durables grew a total of 116 percent while spending on nondurables grew a total of 34 percent (Balke and Gordon 1986). This rapid growth of spending on durables, reflecting households' purchases of autos and appliances, greatly changed the proportions spent on the different consumption components. In 1921 spending on services and nondurables was fifteen times greater than spending on durables; by 1929 it was about nine times greater. (For comparison, in 1991 it was seven times greater.)

Investment spending boomed during the decade as well. Of special note was the enormous rise in spending on both business and residential structures. Investment in business structures peaked at roughly equal values in both 1925 and 1929, and these inflation-adjusted levels were not reached again until 1953. Residential construction peaked in 1928 at inflation-adjusted levels not reattained until 1947.

What factors contributed to the construction boom of the 1920s? The residential construction boom was certainly partly to satisfy pent-up demand generated by low building rates during and shortly after World War I. During the war resources were diverted toward military uses, and then immediately after the war mortgage financing was difficult to obtain (Bolch et al. 1971). When financing finally became readily available, home building boomed. The automobile, too, was important, because it

TABLE 2.1.   Changes in Aggregate Demand and Output, 1920–29

Year	Real GNP Growth (%)	Changes in (Billions of 1929$)				
		GNP	C	I	G	X-M
1920	−1.2	−0.9	2.5	2.1	−4.1	−1.2
1921	−2.3	−1.7	3.4	−5.4	0.9	−0.8
1922	5.7	4.2	2.0	3.2	−0.1	−0.8
1923	12.4	10.0	5.3	5.0	−0.1	−0.2
1924	3.0	2.6	4.7	−3.2	0.6	0.5
1925	2.3	2.1	−2.0	4.0	0.5	−0.3
1926	6.3	5.9	5.4	0.7	0.0	−0.3
1927	0.9	0.9	1.7	−1.5	0.5	0.3
1928	1.2	1.2	1.6	−1.1	0.3	0.3
1929	5.8	5.9	4.1	1.7	0.3	−0.2
Totals		30.2	28.7	5.5	−1.2	−2.7

Source: U.S. Department of Commerce 1966.

Note: In some cases the changes in consumption, investment, government purchases, and net exports may not sum to the change in GNP due to rounding errors.

allowed people to move to outlying areas where the first big subdivisions were being built. Yet another factor was the building cycle of 18 to 22 years, which was based on cycles in population growth. A peak in this cycle was apparently hit during the mid-1920s (see, for example, Hughes 1987). Finally, several investigators have claimed that the housing market had a speculative element to it that resulted in an overbuilt market by the late 1920s. For example, Bolch et al. contend that speculative overbuilding is demonstrated by the fact that from 1918 to 1926 net household formation exceeded housing starts, while from 1926 to 1929 housing starts exceeded net household formation (1971).[2] Gordon and Veitch argue that a speculative element is demonstrated by the fact that from 1924 to 1927 the ratio of residential construction to GNP was "by far its highest level of the twentieth century" (1986, 326). Field points out that optimistic entrepreneurs were so busy subdividing acreage into building lots during the 1920s that after the crash in home building America was awash in vacant building lots: "In New Jersey alone . . . [there was] enough prematurely subdivided acreage in 1936 to supply over a million 6,000-square-foot lots, one for every family then resident in the state" (1992, 790–91). It was also estimated that nationally there were roughly as many vacant building lots as there were occupied homes.

A similar boom occurred in business structures. Much of this construction was of office buildings as the growth of large firms required larger buildings to house their employees. At the same time, the development of safe and reliable elevators allowed far taller buildings to be built than had been built before. So in cities, especially New York, many very large office buildings were built, the Empire State Building being the outstanding example.[3] Another factor in the nonresidential construction boom was the building of electrical generating plants to help meet the increasing demand for electricity in urban areas.

Government purchases were stimulative at the state and local level, but at the federal level spending in 1929 was below the level of 1921 (Hughes 1987, 431). A good part of state and local spending went for road construction to meet the increased demand caused by the proliferation of automobiles, as well as for sewer construction in the expanding residential areas.

2.2.   Problems Ahead?

In the midst of this 1920s prosperity were two features that many argue were dark clouds on the horizon: the worsening distribution of income and the stock market boom. The distribution-of-income problem refers to the fact that while most people were becoming better off, those at the top of the income scale were becoming relatively much more affluent than those in lower income brackets. For example, Hughes cites figures showing that the share of total income accruing to the top 1.0 percent of income earners rose from 12 percent in 1922 to 13.7 percent in 1929 (1987, 428–30). Over that same period, the share of wealth held by the top 1 percent of adults rose from 32 percent to 38 percent. In 1922 the top 1 percent of income recipients accounted for 49 percent of total U.S. saving; by 1929 they accounted for 80 percent of saving. Williamson and Lindert report that using any of a number of measures of income inequality, the period of 1928 and the first three quarters of 1929 may include one of "the highest income inequalities in American history" (1980, 75).

Williamson and Lindert contend that the cause of this increased income inequality was the high rate of unbalanced technological progress during the period, that is, laborsaving technological innovations that favored one group of workers over another (1980). During the 1920s, laborsaving technological innovations were concentrated in manufacturing. This change caused a relative demand shift for labor, toward more skilled labor and away from unskilled labor. The laborsaving capital being put into use was replacing jobs at the unskilled level (assembly-line workers) while creating jobs at more skilled levels (for example, machine repairmen). Thus, wages of skilled workers rose relative to those of unskilled workers. Williamson and Lindert conclude that the technological progress during the 1920s raised the skilled labor wage premium by 0.98 percent per year (1980, 247).

Another important factor helping cause the changing distributions of income and wealth were the changes occurring in the functional distribution of income. Wages grew more slowly than output per worker, which suggests that corporate profits were rising. This change shows up as rising dividends, which constituted 4.3 percent of national income in 1920 and rose to 7.2 percent of national income by 1929 (Soule 1947, 284). Since 82 percent of all dividends were paid to the top 5 percent of income earners, this clearly helped contribute to the change in income inequality (Potter 1974).

This increased inequality of both income and wealth has been blamed by various people for helping cause the Great Depression. This argument, often associated with the underconsumptionist school of thought, notes that higher-income individuals have lower average propensities to consume than do lower-income individuals.[4] Thus, when increasing proportions of income are placed in the hands of higher-income individuals, the aggregate average propensity to consume falls. This argument has been applied to the late 1920s; underconsumptionists contend that as the distribution of income worsened, the average propensity to consume fell. Thus, aggregate demand growth was below what it would have been had the distribution of income remained stable.[5]

Many writers describe this process as being instrumental in setting off the recession in 1929. Hughes argues that the end of the building construction boom in the late 1920s occurred as "demand simply died off, slowly but remorselessly. It was not the case that the country was suffering from an excess of housing, but, *given the distribution of family incomes,* demand was exhausted" (1987, 434). Faulkner, commenting on the relationship between the worsening income and wealth distribution and the economic collapse in 1929, contends that the problem was "the tendency to pile up wealth where it would be used chiefly for further expansion of industrial units rather than to place it in the hands of those who would use it to purchase manufactured commodities" (1960, 642). Potter claims that "the failure to redistribute incomes, especially towards the end of the 1920s, must be held to have been instrumental in holding consumption down below its fullest potential and . . . to have increased saving at a time when the economy required even further increases in spending" (1974, 68).

While there is little doubt that the distribution of income and wealth became more unequal during the 1920s, it is not clear just how much this change had to do with initiating and causing the Great Depression. Clearly those people sympathetic with the underconsumptionist view think that it had a great deal to do with causing the economic problems of the 1930s. But critics of that view contend that increased inequality of income and wealth is an unlikely candidate to cause an economic decline on the order of the Great Depression. Their criticism of the underconsumptionist view is that it ignores an obvious adjustment mechanism; if deficient demand for goods and services is caused by unequal distribution of income, then the price level would fall to cause the quantity of goods and services demanded to rise. Underconsumptionists respond that prices could not fall because of various rigidities built into the economic system (see, for example, Stricker 1983–84).

The second major problem in the minds of many was the stock market boom during the late 1920s. During much of the 1920s stock prices rose significantly, but especially during the last three years of the decade. Using Balke and Gordon's (1986) index of common stock prices, equity values rose 27 percent in 1922, fell 7 percent in 1923, and then rose 16 percent in 1924, 27 percent in 1925, 5 percent in 1926, 25 percent in 1927, 29 percent in 1928, and finally another 30 percent during 1929 up to the peak in September. Certainly holding stocks during the 1920s was a good investment: if an individual had bought a representative basket of stocks at the economic trough in 1921.III and had the sagacity to sell at the peak in September 1929 they would have earned a return of 412 percent *excluding dividend payments!* Furthermore, since the price level was falling slightly during that period, the real return would have been even higher.

According to several accounts, the stock market boom on Wall Street generated a great deal of excitement among Americans. While a relatively small number of people were directly involved in the market, only around 1.0 percent of the U.S. population according to Galbraith (1954, 78), Americans got caught up in the mood of the times. Consider the comments of a major commentator of that era, the great social historian Frederick Lewis Allen:

The speculative fever was infecting the whole country. Stories of fortunes made overnight were on everybody's lips. One financial commentator reported that his doctor found patients talking about the market to the exclusion of everything else and that his barber was punctuating with the hot towel more than one account of the prospects of Montgomery Ward. Wives were asking their husbands why they were so slow, why they weren't getting in on all this, only to hear that their husbands had bought a hundred shares of American Linseed that very morning. (1931, 210)

Or what the noted historian William Leuchtenburg says about the market's effect on the general public:

Even by the summer of 1929 the market had drawn people who never dreamed they would be caught in the speculative frenzy. How much longer could you hold out when your neighbor who bought General Motors at 99 in 1925 sold it at 212 in 1928? There were stories of a plunger who entered the market with a million dollars and ran it up to thirty millions in eight months, of a peddler who parlayed $4,000 into $250,000. The Bull Market was not simply a phenomenon of New York and Chicago; there were brokerage offices in towns like Steubenville, Ohio and Storm Lake, Iowa. Even non-investors followed the market news; like batting averages, it touched the statistical heart of the country. (1958, 243)

A great deal of energy has been spent trying to determine the cause(s) of this late 1920s stock market boom, and explanations generally fall into one of two categories: either (1) the stock market boom was a speculative bubble that would eventually burst, or (2) the stock price gains were based on solid fundamentals and so the 1929 crash was not inevitable.

The most notable proponent of the bubble-waiting-to-burst view is Galbraith (1954). He argues that four factors suggest that the market had a large speculative element to it. First is the sheer size of the stock price gains in 1928 and 1929. As noted earlier, equity values rose 29 percent in 1928 and another 30 percent in 1929 (to the peak in September). What is notable about the 30 percent rise during 1929 is that 25 percentage points of it occurred during just the months of June, July, and August.

The second factor is the volume of transactions. On many days during 1929 between four and five million shares were traded, a much higher daily volume than had been traded before. On an annual basis, 582 million shares were traded in 1927, then 931 million in 1928 and 1,125 million in 1929 (Federal Reserve Board of Governors 1943, 485).

Third was the combination of the enormous growth of corporations' loans to brokers and the willingness of shareholders to pay much higher rates on borrowings from brokers than were being earned on stocks. Brokers borrowed from banks and nonfinancial corporations (called brokers' loans) and then lent the funds to individuals to purchase equity shares in margin accounts.[6] These brokers' loans grew enormously during the mid- and late 1920s. Loans to brokers totaled $7.63 billion in 1924 and then rose to $26.53 billion by 1929. Brokers turned around and lent these funds to individuals in margin accounts. From January 1929 up to the crash that began in September, weekly rates on these margin loans ranged from 6.00 percent to 14.4 percent. For 1929 as a whole, the dividend yield on stocks averaged 3.48 percent. At the market's peak in September 1929 the dividend yield on stocks was 2.92 percent while weekly rates on margin loans averaged 8.56 percent. In other words, individuals were paying 8.56 percent to borrow to buy stocks paying dividend yields averaging 2.92 percent. Galbraith implies that speculation was evident because people holding margin accounts must have been expecting strong gains in stock prices to make paying such rates profitable.[7] Along similar lines, Rappaport and White argue that speculation is suggested in 1929 because rates on brokers' loans rose significantly above other short-term rates, which they attribute to very high demand for margin loans (1994).[8]

Finally, Galbraith argues that yet another indicator of speculative activity was the public's willingness to purchase shares of the highly leveraged investment trusts that were developed during the 1920s. He describes how the investment trusts worked by considering one with an initial capitalization of $150 million raised in the following way:

$50 million — debt
$50 million — preferred stock
$50 million — common stock

The investment trust would then use the $150 million to buy shares of stocks of various corporations listed on the exchange. Any appreciation in prices of the shares purchased by the trust would accrue to the common stockholders of the trust because the debt (bonds issued) had a fixed nominal value and the preferred stock had a stated maximum dividend that would be paid. Thus, any increase in value of the trust's holdings would not alter the value of the bonds or preferred stock, but would all accrue to the value of the common stock. Suppose the value of the stocks held by the trust rose by 50 percent, which would have happened during the late 1920s in something over a year. If the holdings of $150 million rose by 50 percent, they would be worth $225 million, and the entire gain of $75 million would accrue to the trust's common stockholders. So the value of their stock would rise from $50 million to $125 million, a gain of 150 percent. This is nothing more than the concept of leverage in action; since two-thirds of the trust was capitalized with debt and preferred stock, the common stockholders fare very well as long as equity prices are rising. Of course, the common stockholders would fare quite poorly if the values of the stocks held by the trust fell.

The problem, according to Galbraith, was not the trusts as such, but the fact that the trusts held the stocks of other leveraged trusts. Suppose there was a second trust that was identical to the first trust in that it was capitalized in exactly the same way ($50 million each of debt, preferred stock, and common stock) but used the $150 million to buy not a portfolio of various stocks listed on the exchange, but instead only common stocks of other investment trusts just like the first one discussed. If this second investment trust held common stock of trusts like the first one, the return on the second trust's holdings would be 150 percent (the rise in the first trust's common stock value), all of which would accrue to the common stock of the second trust. Since the second trust originally bought $150 million of such stock, a 150 percent gain on $150 million translates into a gain of $225 million, *all accruing to the original $50 million of the second trust's common stock*. Thus, the value of the stock of the second trust would go from $50 million to $275 million, a gain of 450 percent. It does not stop there. If a third investment trust existed that held the stock of trusts like the second one, then the return on the common stock of the third trust would be even bigger yet, 1050 percent.

Given these exceptional returns, Wall Street firms developed investment trusts at a furious pace: "during 1928 an estimated 186 investment trusts were organized; by early 1929 they were being promoted at the rate of approximately one each business day" (Galbraith 1954, 49). These trusts sold about $400 million worth of securities in 1927, and by 1929 they sold about $3 billion, which amounted to about one-third of all new financial capital raised that year (Galbraith 1954, 50). In Galbraith's view the public's willingness to purchase shares of these investment trusts provides further evidence that the stock gains of the late 1920s were a house of cards waiting to fall. When the stock market crashed, the geometric magic of leveraged price gains worked in reverse to generate enormous price declines. He documents one case of the Goldman Sachs Trading Corporation, which was a leveraged investment trust that owned shares of several other investment trusts. Its stock price went from $104 per share in 1928 to $1.75 in 1932 (1954, 65).

Shiller agrees with Galbraith's conclusion that stock prices in 1929 were based on speculation, but provides different evidence to support his conclusion (1981). He notes that the price of a stock is the discounted present value of the expected future dividends, or

$$P_s = D1/(1 + r) + D2/(1 + r)^2 + D3/(1 + r)^3 + \ldots + Dn/(1 + r)^n$$

where P_s is the price of the stock, Di is the dividend expected to be received in the ith year, r is the discount rate, and the stock is expected to pay dividends for n years. Since the dividend terms in the equation are expected values, errors of expectations will be present. Thus, we can note that the true price of the stock, P_s, will be equal to the expected value, which we denote P^e, plus an expectational error, u, or

$$P_s = P^e + u.$$

Since stockholders are assumed to incorporate all currently available information into their forecasted value, any expectational errors are expected to be independent of the value of P^s or P^e. Thus, the relationship between the variances of the three variables is as follows:

$$\text{Var}(P_s) = \text{Var}(P^e) + \text{Var}(u)$$

Since the lowest possible value for a variance is zero, it must be true that $\text{Var}(P_s) \leq \text{Var}(P^e)$, or in terms of standard deviations,[9]

$$\text{SD}(P_s) \leq \text{SD}(P^e).$$

This presents us with a testable hypothesis, that if a stock price is the present value of the expected dividends, then the variability of actual stock prices (measured by the standard deviation) should be less than or equal to the variability of the present value of the expected dividends. Of course, we can not directly measure expected dividends, so Shiller proxies them with actual realized dividends. In other words, the test is carried out by computing the standard deviation of actual stock prices and the standard deviation of the present value of actual dividends received, and then comparing them. He finds that for the Dow Jones Industrial Average, the variability of stock prices in 1929 was nearly two times higher than the variability of discounted dividends. This result suggests two possibilities to Shiller: either investors were acting irrationally in 1929 by bidding prices up far in excess of the amount suggested by expected dividends, or the stock market boom and crash was nothing more than a really huge error of forecasting dividends. Shiller accepts the former possibility and dismisses the latter. He contends that since the variability of the stock price series has repeatedly risen well above the present value of dividends over a series of decades, it seems highly unlikely that investors would keep making huge errors forecasting dividends. Instead, his conclusion is that stock prices in 1929 were formed irrationally, dominated by speculative behavior.

Not all are convinced that the 1920s stock market was a bubble waiting to burst. There are many who contend that the gains in stock prices were quite reasonable given the fundamentals of the mid- and late 1920s. This view contends that the crash in prices was quite unexpected and hardly inevitable. For example, Hughes notes that stock yields were not that much different from bond yields in 1928 when the Federal Reserve began expressing great concern about stock market speculation (1987). Not until 1929 did yields on utilities stocks fall below, and yields on industrial stocks become roughly equal to, yields on U.S. Treasury bonds. In those terms, stock prices may have been overpriced in 1929, but certainly not in 1928.

Sirkin (1975) and Bierman (1991) contend that stock prices were not overvalued in 1929 either. Both apply a formula developed by Malkiel (1963) to explain the relationship between stock prices, earnings, earnings growth, and the discount rate. Sirkin (1975) uses the 29 profitable firms out of the 30 used to compute the Dow Jones Industrial Average in 1929.[10] The mean price–earnings ratio for these firms' stocks at the market's peak in September 1929 was 21.6 while the median value was 15.1. Assuming very reasonable values for the interest rate at the time, Sirkin finds that for the price–earnings ratio of 15 to be maintained, earnings growth of 6.0 percent would have been required for the next five to ten years. The actual earnings growth for those same 29 stocks had averaged 8.0 percent from 1925 to 1929. In other words, if investors expected earnings to continue growing from 1929 to 1934 at a rate similar to what had occurred from 1925 to 1929, then the stock prices prevailing in September 1929 were very much in line with fundamentals. Sirkin considers such growth in line with expectations given the general optimism of 1929. He concludes, "[these] price earnings ratios [of the 29 stocks] . . . hardly present a picture of a 'speculative orgy' in 'a time of madness.' At least half of the twenty nine participants appear to have been cold sober. Some showed signs of over-indulgence. But, by the usual standards of such things, the conclusion would have to be: not much of an orgy" (Sirkin 1975, 231). Using similar analysis, Bierman reaches essentially the same conclusion (1991).

Santoni investigates the proposition that the stock market of the 1920s was a rational bubble (1987). A rational bubble describes an asset price that rises above the price dictated by fundamentals, that is, above the price suggested by earnings and interest rates on alternative assets. An asset price would rise above the price suggested by fundamentals to compensate holders for the additional risk they take on. For this reason, prices that are following a rational bubble would tend to be autocorrelated over time and to lie above the mean value for a prolonged period. Santoni tests this hypothesis and concludes that stock prices were not autocorrelated during 1928 and 1929 up to the market peak in early September. Therefore, he concludes that stock prices did not follow the pattern of a bubble prior to the crash.[11]

So the jury is still out on whether the stock market advance of the late 1920s was due to speculative excess or to fundamentals. Reaching a verdict on this question is important because it has significant implications for the nature of the crash in October. If the stock prices were based on irrational overspeculation then the implication is that the crash was the natural result of excesses during the 1920s and by implication the ensuing output declines may have been partly the result of the 1920s speculation. In other words, the Great Depression would have been, in fact, "payback time" for the exceptional but undeserved prosperity that preceded it. On the other hand, if the stock market rise was based on fundamentals, then the crash and by implication the Great Depression were not inevitable.

2.3. The Federal Reserve's Reaction

The Federal Reserve made it perfectly clear what they thought about the stock market boom: it represented excessive speculation and, as such, should be stopped. They were particularly concerned about the role member banks were playing in helping fuel the perceived speculation. The Federal Reserve began expressing concern in early 1928 and at that time began a policy of monetary restriction in an effort to stem the stock market advance. This policy continued through May 1929. The monetary restriction was carried out by selling $405 million in government securities and raising the discount rate in three stages from 3.5 percent to 5 percent at all Federal Reserve banks. They explained why they were doing this in the February 1929 issue of their official mouthpiece, the *Federal Reserve Bulletin*. There they reprinted a letter that was sent from the Federal Reserve Board to all twelve Federal Reserve banks. It reads in part:

———◦◦◦———

The extraordinary absorption of funds in speculative security loans, which has characterized the credit movement during the past year or more, in the judgement of the Federal Reserve Board, deserves particular attention lest it become a decisive factor working toward a still further firming of money rates to the prejudice of the country's commercial interests.

The Federal reserve act does not, in the opinion of the Federal Reserve Board, contemplate the use of the resources of the Federal reserve banks for the creation of speculative credit. A member bank is not within its reasonable claims for rediscount facilities at its Federal reserve bank when it borrows either for the purpose of making speculative loans or for the purpose of maintaining speculative loans.

The board has no disposition to assume authority to interfere with the loan practices of member banks so long as they do not involve the Federal reserve banks. It has, however, a grave responsibility whenever there is evidence that member banks are maintaining speculative security loans with the aid of Federal reserve credit. When such is the case the Federal reserve bank becomes either a contributing or a sustaining factor in the current volume of speculative security credit. This is not in harmony with the intent of the Federal reserve act, nor is it conducive to the wholesome operation of the banking and credit system of the country. (94)

So it is clear that the Federal Reserve Board was quite concerned with the stock market advance, and this is why they pursued the contractionary monetary policy beginning in 1928. Economists across the intellectual spectrum, from monetarists like Friedman and Schwartz (1963) to Keynesians such as Temin (1989) agree that this restrictive monetary policy initiated by the Federal Reserve Board in response to the stock market boom was the cause of the initial economic slowdown that eventually turned into the Great Depression.

CHAPTER 3

The Gold Standard

The discussion in chapter 2 may suggest to readers that the Federal Reserve's monetary policy during the 1920s was being conducted in isolation from the rest of the world. In fact, international considerations played a major role. But before we discuss the economic conditions in other countries, readers must be familiar with the international monetary standard in place at the time: the gold standard. The existence of the gold standard linked economic conditions across countries to a much greater extent than is currently the case, and it is because of this linkage that the Depression was a worldwide event.

3.1. How the Gold Standard Was Set Up

The reason a [gold] standard works so well is because it is democratic. This may sound like a strange way of putting it, but when the government agrees to maintain the value of the currency it produces, the people are in charge of the money supply.

If one commodity (money) is fixed to gold . . . , the dollar value of all other commodities is more or less fixed . . . inflation would be stopped in its tracks.

We must restore a monetary standard.
                    —*Jack Kemp (1979, 100, 112, and 114)*

Few reading this have ever lived in a world in which gold was money, or even the official backing for our money. It is a measure of the mystical power of its hold over the U.S. economy that six decades after the end of the U.S. system of gold money, called the gold standard, the Republican Electoral Platform of 1980 and 1984 called for its restoration. More recently, the retired Vice Chairman of the Federal Reserve, Wayne Angell, called for a gold standard in Russia to save the ruble from collapse (1989). And in 1996, Steve Forbes framed his run for the U.S. presidency with a call for a flat tax and the return of the United States to the gold standard.

In today's world of paper money controlled by the Federal Reserve, it is hard even to imagine a time in which gold was money and money could not simply be printed at the discretion of the Federal Reserve. To truly understand the economic world of the 1920s and 1930s, it is necessary to understand the gold standard; how it was constructed, how it worked, its advantages and disadvantages, and how it influenced the thinking and behavior of government officials, Wall Street tycoons, and the average man on the street.

Even those who are suspicious of the power of government usually recognize that monetary systems are a proper sphere of influence for government. In fact, this is an area in which we usually concede to government a large degree of monopoly over the production and control of the currency. In the classic gold standard the government had an important role, but it was limited to a few specific functions. The free market was perhaps much more important than government to the functioning of this monetary system, both domestically and internationally. The end result of this fact was that the government could not determine the domestic money supply, *if the rules of the game were followed.*

Domestically, the government's role was to do just three things:

1. Choose and set the price of gold in domestic monetary units. The price of gold in the United States in the period before the Great Depression was fixed at approximately $20 per ounce of gold. Thus, when the U.S. Mint produced gold coins, a $20 coin or gold piece had an ounce of pure gold. There was also one-half ounce of gold in $10 pieces and one-quarter ounce in $5 pieces.

2. In order that the public would believe and accept the set price (as we will see, for good reason it was usually set above what would be the free market equilibrium price), the government stood ready

to buy any gold offered at the set price. Therefore, no one would be willing to sell at a lower price.

3. The government also stood ready to sell gold to anyone at the set price of $20 per ounce. As a practical matter, this meant that government had to maintain large stocks of gold. This gold was needed not only to meet monetary needs, but also to satisfy any demand for gold to be used commercially in the production of jewelry, in dental work, and even as a catalyst in chemical reactions. There was then, and is today, a huge commercial demand for gold. For example, in 1988 total gold production from U.S. mines was 205.3 tons, or 5.6 million ounces. World production was 1,538 tons. The total quantity of gold used by world industrial fabricators alone was 1,840 tons. Of this, 1,483 tons were used in jewelry, 134 tons in electronics, and 50 tons in dental work (Buckley 1989, 220–21). That same year, 9.5 million futures contracts were sold in the New York commodity market (each contract was for 100 ounces). In 1929, 20.5 million ounces valued at $42.5 million were mined in the United States. Total U.S. monetary gold in 1929 was 193.4 million ounces, which was valued at $3.997 billion.

As a result, the gold standard was an expensive system to operate. Large amounts of resources were tied up in the stocks of U.S. Treasury–owned gold in the form of bullion, or gold bars. Even though we are no longer on a gold monetary standard, in 1993 world governments still held a total of 1.44 billion ounces of gold as official reserves (Knight-Ridder Financial Publishing 1994). The U.S. government still holds 8,000 tons (250 million ounces) of gold in the Federal Reserve Bank of New York and in the Gold Depositories at Fort Knox, Kentucky and West Point, New York.

In the 1920s and 1930s this stock of gold was usually made available to meet the demands of the public and businesses through the simple expedient of allowing anyone who wanted gold to melt down coins that could be obtained at any bank. When there was a large drain of gold from the banks and inventories dropped, the government was expected to accommodate this need passively by sending more gold to banks in exchange for bank assets.

It should be pointed out that paper currency also existed, but mostly in the form of notes that could be exchanged for gold. The government was required to maintain gold backing for all paper currency issued. In 1929, 40 percent backing was required by law. In addition, bank deposits existed, and banks were required to keep gold, currency, or Federal Reserve deposits as reserve backing for these deposits. Thus, when people cashed checks or withdrew savings from banks, the banks lost gold, which represented bank reserves. We will see that the effects of such drains were devastating to the world economy and banking systems after 1929.

The startling implication of having the government follow the rules of the game and limit its monetary responsibilities to the three functions listed above (setting the price of gold and buying and selling it in unlimited amounts to maintain the price) was that the government could not control the domestic money supply. This may be a shocking idea to modern minds.

3.2. Determination of the Money Supply under the Gold Standard

The domestic money supply was in reality based upon the residual of the total amount of gold supplied to the economy and the amount of gold demanded for commercial and industrial purposes. This is illustrated in figure 3.1, which represents the market for the gold stock using a simple supply and demand analysis. The axes of the graph express the price of gold and the quantity available in the market. The commercial demand for gold, $D0$, slopes down and to the right, expressing the fact that the quantity demanded increases as its price falls (for example, as jewelry is made less expensive to buy, the quantity demanded rises). The supply of gold, $S0$, slopes upward to the right, expressing the fact that producers of gold will have an incentive to mine and sell more gold in the market as the price rises and, therefore, the profits to the firm increase as revenues from additional production also increase.

Normally, we would expect the price of gold in a free market to be at *Pe,* the equilibrium price that equates supply and demand in the market. However, under the gold standard this market was not the purely competitive market that would have produced this result. Remember, the government was involved as a dominant force in the market. As discussed above, the government fixed the price of gold and bought and sold gold in unlimited quantities in order to maintain the price that they themselves had chosen. They were able to maintain this price because of the tremendously large stocks of gold they held and stood ready to sell, and

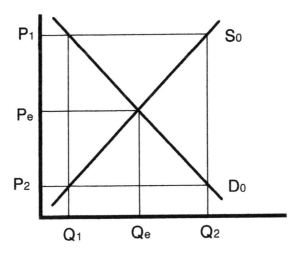

Fig. 3.1.   The market for gold

the huge amounts that they could buy using their enormous financial resources.

But which price would they chose? Would it be *Pe?* Or would it be *P*1 as shown in figure 3.1, a price higher than equilibrium, or *P2*, a lower price? Because the public had the right to melt down coins to obtain the gold they wanted, the demanders of commercial gold had first claim on the available stocks. Therefore, at a price at or below *Pe,* no gold would be available to serve as the nation's domestic money supply because there would be no excess supply, that is, the entire gold stock would be in commercial use. Thus, the government chose a price above *Pe* to set and maintain because a price above *Pe* would ensure an excess supply—gold left over that is not used by commercial buyers.

Note that at *P*1 the gold money supply, the supply of gold in excess of commercial demand, is measured by the distance between *Q*1 and *Q*2. Note also that at any point in time, the size of the domestic money supply would be larger as the price chosen by the government became higher.

Once the price of gold was chosen and then fixed at that level through purchases and sales in the market, the government had no further function in the operation of the gold standard. In fact, the more important point is the reality that once this price was set, the government had no further control over the money supply. The money supply was determined by increases or decreases in either the commercial demand for gold or the quantities of gold supplied to the economy.

For example, suppose a fad had swept the nation in 1927 because Calvin Coolidge appeared in public wearing one gold earring. Then every teenager in America wanted to wear a gold earring "just like silent Cal." (It could have happened!) The result would be a shift to the right in the commercial demand for gold (for example, to $D1$ in figure 3.2). Since more gold would be used in earrings, less would be available for money. The commercial use of gold would become $Q3$, and the money supply would become $Q2 - Q3$, instead of $Q2 - Q1$ as was the case before. It would be beyond the power of government to do anything about this fact. What a scary thought: the teenagers of America would have caused the U.S. money supply to decline!

When this possibility is considered, it seems amazing that the gold standard still retains the support of a large group of grown-ups. We have pointed out that Steve Forbes ran for the Republican nomination for president in 1996 with the return to a gold standard as an important plank in his platform. To be fair, Mr. Forbes, or Jack Kemp before him, probably did not have in mind the pure gold standard of 100 years ago. But still, allowing teenagers to control the money supply?

Shifts in the supply schedule could impact the money supply as well. Suppose a historic gold strike was made by miners in California in 1848, or Alaska in 1896. The effect in figure 3.3 would be dramatic. The supply of gold, $S0$, would increase to $S1$, and the U.S. Treasury would have had to passively buy any gold offered to it by miners at $P1$. The money supply would expand from $Q2 - Q1$ to $Q3 - Q1$.

The strength of the gold standard was its stability and, therefore, the stability of the value of money. It is this characteristic that produced the trust in our money that the public had then, and that explains the nostalgia for the gold standard that remains today. Except for minor adjustments, and the temporary suspensions of gold payments during wartimes, the price of gold was held constant from the establishment of the new United States of America in 1791 until gold was revalued in 1933.

3.3. International Implications

One important feature that emerged from the gold standard was the existence of fixed exchange rates between currencies of countries on the gold standard. For example, the United States set the official price of gold at $1 per 23.22 grains.[1] Britain set their official price of gold at 1 pound per 113 grains. Since gold could be readily bought and sold in both countries

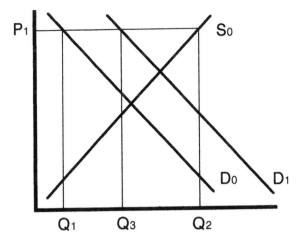

Fig. 3.2.   Effect of an increase in the demand for gold

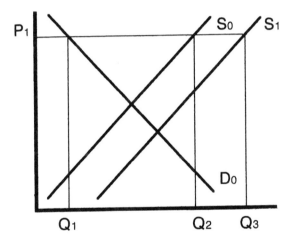

Fig. 3.3.   Effect of an increase in the supply of gold

at these official prices, it follows that once adjusted for the exchange rate between the dollar and pound, the value of gold should be the same in both countries. Since the price of gold should be the same in both countries, we can form a ratio (called the *parity ratio*):

113 grains/pound / 23.22 grains/dollar = (113 grains/23.22 grains) × (dollar/pound) = 4.86 dollars/pound

which was the exchange rate between the dollar and the pound under the gold standard.

The best way to understand why this exchange rate resulted is to see what would happen if the exchange rate were not $4.86/pound. For example, suppose the exchange rate were $5.00/pound. At this exchange rate someone could spend $1 in the United States and buy 23.22 grains of gold. Then they could take the gold across the ocean to Britain and sell it for .205 pounds (23.22/113 = .205). Next, they would ship their British pounds back to the U.S. and sell their .205 pounds on the foreign currency market for $1.025 (= .205 pounds × $5/pound). Thus, they converted $1 into $1.025! Of course, if such a profit opportunity existed, profiteers would not be moving a few grains across the ocean, they would be moving gold in large amounts and pocketing significant profits. As they did so the demand for U.S. dollars would rise (because they were buying gold in the United States with dollars) while the supply of pounds would increase (because they were selling the gold in Britain for pounds and then using them to buy dollars in the U.S.). Thus, the dollar would rise in value relative to the pound and the exchange rate would fall back toward $4.86/pound. This process would continue as long as profit opportunities existed, which would be the case as long as the exchange rate varied more than a cent or two from $4.86/pound (a penny or two was roughly the cost of shipping a British pound's worth of gold across the Atlantic Ocean). Therefore, the actions of individuals seeking profits (arbitrageurs) would produce fixed exchange rates over very long periods of time.

Another important international aspect of the gold standard was the ability of the free flow of gold between countries to correct imbalances in the flow of payments between nations. The balance of payments between nations is very important because imbalances generate problems in financing trade. For example, when Americans import goods from Britain they are expected to pay for them with British currency. After all, a British firm does not want to be paid in dollars, they want pounds. Thus, a major complication of international trade is that trade between countries involves two currencies. Where do people get this foreign currency? In this case of British trade, Americans need pounds. They can get them in three ways: (1) borrow them, (2) sell other assets to buy them, or (3) earn them.

In the long run, borrowing and selling assets is a limited solution, so it ultimately comes down to earning them. How? Through the sale of U.S. goods (exports) to Britain. The balance of payments tells us whether Americans are exporting more or less than they are importing, and this indicates whether the United States is earning enough pounds from exports to Britain to continue to pay for the imported goods they desire.

In the example above in which the exchange rate had risen to $5/pound before being driven back down toward $4.86/pound, the short-run rise in the exchange rate indicates that the demand for pounds to pay for imports had risen relative to the supply generated from U.S. exports. In other words, the United States had a deficit in its balance while Britain had a surplus.

In the short run, this U.S. deficit was covered by arbitrageurs bringing in British pounds as they pursued profits by shipping gold from the United States to Britain. In essence, the United States sold assets (gold) to get the needed pounds. In an accounting sense the U.S. balance of payments and the supply and demand of pounds *were made to balance,* but in an economic sense the United States merely papered over its shortage of pounds. If nothing had changed in U.S. behavior, in the next period the United States would again be using its national wealth (gold) to buy consumer goods from Britain. Americans would be living off their savings. Thus, an adjustment in the imbalance was necessary in the long run to insure that the United States could continue to pay for its imports.

The United States could borrow the pounds to eliminate the payments deficit, and, as we will see, in the 1930s this was one solution used by governments. Another option would be for the United States to raise interest rates. By doing so, the United States could induce foreigners to put their savings in U.S. banks and financial assets to earn these higher interest rates. Foreigners would buy dollars with pounds in order to open U.S. bank accounts, and U.S. currency markets would be supplied with pounds. However, the higher interest rates necessary to bring this about would also cause reductions in U.S. investment, inventory accumulation, and consumption, which would adversely affect output and employment in the United States. Another drawback of attracting foreign investment is that in the event of a financial crisis, British investors could pull these funds out of the United States and take them back to Britain quite suddenly and unexpectedly.

Instead, the gold standard supplied a solution to the payment adjustment problem. The free movement of gold, and thus money, between countries tended automatically to produce long-run economic balance in international payments through changes in imports and exports. For example, if the United States exported more than it imported, it would have a surplus of receipts over payments. This seems like a great situation. Money would be flowing into the country. Jobs in the export industries would be high and increasing, and, therefore, incomes would also be rising.

However, the United States' trading partners would not be in such a fine position. Because they were buying more U.S. goods than Americans were buying from them, the U.S. surplus implies a deficit for the other countries. This would mean money and gold were flowing out of the deficit countries. A decline in their money supplies would cause a decline in the demand for goods in those countries, thus causing falling prices and incomes. This is something that no country could, or would, endure over the long run.

Fortunately, the free flow of gold and money if left alone would automatically correct the problem, and it is for this reason that the rules of the game were devised. As more money flowed into the United States because of their surplus and was made available to spend, the demand for goods by the American public would also rise, and therefore, U.S. prices would tend to rise relative to foreign prices. This would make U.S. goods less competitive with foreign imported goods. As time passed, U.S. and foreign consumers would recognize this fact and buy fewer U.S. goods and more of the cheaper foreign goods. The net effect would be for U.S. exports to fall and imports to rise, thus reducing the U.S. surplus.

When enough gold flowed into the U.S. and raised prices enough, the United States would eventually expect to experience a deficit. This implies that the United States' trading partners would also experience a correction of their deficit, and it would be transformed into a surplus. No one country would expect to face a continual deficit and the perpetual burden of a loss of gold and falling prices. There was instead a continual movement toward balance in international payments that over time automatically solved the deficit problems. But for this process to work, governments had to keep their hands off and let the system work, that is, *they had to play by the rules of the game.*

3.4.   What If the Rules Were Broken?

Suppose that, for some reason, a government decided to interfere. In particular, consider the possibility of one country deciding to not allow their gold flow to impact upon their money supply. How could they do this? It

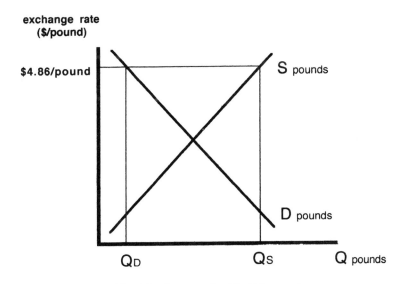

exchange rate ($/pound)

$4.86/pound

S pounds

D pounds

Q_D   Q_S   Q pounds

Fig. 3.4. An overvalued British pound

is simple: conduct an open market operation to offset the gold flow! Suppose, for example, that $1 million worth of gold flowed into the United States from another country, say Britain. If both governments stood by passively, then the monetary base in the United States would rise by $1 million and the monetary base in Britain would fall by $1 million worth of British pounds, which would have been a little over 200,000 pounds in 1929. In this case, the self-adjustment mechanism described above would have worked unhindered.

However, suppose instead that the U.S. central bank, the Federal Reserve, decided to sell U.S. government bonds worth $1 million in the New York financial markets at the same time the $1 million worth of gold flowed in. The effect of this sale would be to reduce bank reserves by $1 million. In this case the monetary base in the United States would remain constant; the gold inflow added $1 million to the base, but the bond sale reduced the base by $1 million. The net effect on the U.S. money supply would be zero. This process is called sterilization. Yet, assuming the Bank of England did not buy any bonds when the gold flowed out of that country (because they were following the rules), their monetary base would still fall by 200,000 pounds. The impact on the system is that Britain bears the brunt of the adjustment. Since the money supply in the United States did not rise, neither did U.S. incomes and prices as they were supposed to, which would have helped Britain eliminate their payments deficit. Since Britain was not aided by rising exports to the United States, Britain must experience a more severe decline in its incomes and prices than would have been the case if the U.S. money supply had gone up. In this way, Britain would bear the brunt of the adjustment in the form of a more severe recession than would have occurred if the United States had been playing by the rules. Thus, it was critical that each country play fair.

Unfortunately, as we will see in the next chapter, the scenario just described did, in fact, occur during the 1920s and was a major factor in the sequence of events that generated the Great Depression. In 1925 Britain returned to the gold standard at the pre–World War I parity ratio.[2] This implied that the exchange rate between the U.S. dollar and the British pound would be $4.86/pound. However, this exchange rate was about 10 percent too high, that is, the British pound was overvalued by about 10 percent relative to the U.S. dollar. The situation is shown in figure 3.4 where the overvalued pound resulted in an excess supply of pounds (excess demand for dollars) on currency markets, which indicates that Britain had a payments deficit. This payments deficit resulted in a gold outflow from Britain to both the United States and France, and, according to the rules of the game, the money supplies in both countries should have risen and driven up their price levels. The rising prices would reduce U.S. and French exports to Britain while raising U.S. and French imports from Britain. In this way, the British payments deficit would shrink as would the U.S. and French surpluses.

However, for reasons discussed in the next chapter, both France and the United States broke the rules of the game by sterilizing their gold inflows. As a result, Britain had to bear the brunt of the adjustment by having a more serious recession and larger decline in prices than would have been the case if the United States and France had played by the rules. This ongoing British payments deficit and accompanying gold outflow was a major factor in the sequence of events that helped bring about the worldwide Great Depression.

CHAPTER 4

International Considerations

The origins of the Great Depression lie largely in the disruptions of the First World War.

—*Peter Temin (1989, 1)*

Economic events taking place in several countries, but three in particular, played a large part in the unfolding sequence of events that led to the Great Depression. These three countries are Britain, Germany, and France. We discuss each in turn.

4.1. Britain

At Cambridge [University], where the ratio of women to men had climbed higher and higher as the war depleted the supply of male students, Phyllis Taylor waited, at eleven, for her geology lecturer, Mr. Thomas, to stride in, the tattered skirts of his MA gown dragging on the floor. He arrived at 11:05, ceremoniously extracted his watch, and announced, ignoring the sexual balance of the classroom, "Gentlemen, the Armistice has just been signed. There will be no further lectures in the University today. Good morning." Then he strode out. Outside, students smashed the offices of the *Cambridge Magazine,* the only college periodical that had been pacifist in its policy.

—*Stanley Weintraub (1985, 280)*

4.1.1. War and the Boom

World War I had very unpleasant consequences for Britain. The country lost an estimated 908,000 soldiers to battle casualties and disease, which represented about 2.0 percent of its 1914 population.[1] Output in Britain rose 8.5 percent from 1914 to 1918, but this figure masks a major shift in the composition of output. The economy was very heavily geared toward the war effort with much of Britain's output being for war material. Virtually no new building construction took place during the war, nor were many new consumer durables available. In addition, German submarines destroyed a great deal of cargo bound for Britain, including food. There were severe shortages of many foods during the war, and the government carried out several campaigns to persuade the civilian population to reduce their consumption levels. British civilians suffered greatly from widespread hunger and malnutrition. Inflation was another major problem: the British price level roughly doubled during the war.

Following demilitarization, the British economy began a boom in 1919 that lasted into 1920. A large pent-up demand for business investment goods, residential housing, and consumer durables existed and was satisfied with significant purchasing power that firms and households had accumulated during the war. During 1919 consumer spending rose 21 percent and industrial production by 10 percent. Firms were not able to keep up with demand because the capacity simply was not available. Producers required more time to expand their operations. As a result, prices rose very rapidly; the wholesale price index rose 10.6 percent in 1919 and another 24.4 percent during 1920 (Aldcroft 1970, 32). The boom also had a large speculative element to it. Aldcroft notes that "the outstanding feature of the boom was the extent of the speculative buying in commodities, securities and real estate and the very large number of industrial transactions at inflated prices. Some idea of the dimensions involved can be gained from the following . . . new capital issues on the London money market rose from 65.3 million [pounds] in 1918 to 237.5 million [pounds] in 1919 to a peak of 384.2 million [pounds] in 1920. This figure for 1920 was not reached again until well after the Second World War" (1970, 35).

The boom came to an abrupt halt in 1920, and the economy was in a free fall by 1921. The cause of the decline is debated; Friedman and Schwartz argue that restrictive monetary policy in the United States ended the boom (1963, 237), while Aldcroft contends that the initial cause was an end to the artificial boom associated with speculation, although restrictive monetary policies certainly made it worse (1983, 13). Whatever the case, the decline was severe. From 1920 to 1921 British industrial production fell 18.6 percent, the wholesale price index fell 35.8 percent, and the unemployment rate rose from 3.9 percent to 16.9 percent.[2]

The economy began to recover in late 1921 and expanded quite rapidly for the next few years although the unemployment rate remained high. Table 4.1 shows income growth, the inflation rate, and the unemployment rate for the United Kingdom from 1921 to 1929. Output growth was strong from 1922 to 1925, but then slowed considerably from 1926 to 1929.

4.1.2.   Unemployment and $4.86/pound

The Chancellor of the Exchequer [Winston Churchill] has expressed the opinion that the return to the gold standard is no more responsible for the condition of affairs in the coal industry than is the Gulf Stream. These statements are of the feather-brained order. It is open to Ministers to argue that the restoration of gold is worth the sacrifice and that the sacrifice is temporary.
—*John Maynard Keynes, launching one of his attacks on Winston Churchill for restoring Britain to the gold standard (1925, 245–46)*

The economic slowdown was the result of an ill-fated move by Britain to return to the gold standard at the pre–World War I parity. Winston

TABLE 4.1.   Real Income Growth, Inflation, and the Unemployment Rate, United Kingdom, 1921–29 (in percentages)

Year	Real Income Growth	Inflation Rate	Unemployment Rate
1921	−4.1	−11.9	12.2
1922	3.8	−17.2	10.8
1923	3.8	−8.5	8.9
1924	4.6	−0.9	7.9
1925	6.7	0.7	8.6
1926	−3.9	−1.6	9.6
1927	8.7	−2.6	7.4
1928	1.3	−1.0	8.2
1929	3.6	−0.4	8.0

Source: Real Income and Implicit Price Deflator taken from Friedman and Schwartz 1980, table 4.9. Unemployment rate is total unemployed as a proportion of total employees, taken from Garside 1990, table 2.

Churchill, who was then Chancellor of the Exchequer for Britain (roughly the equivalent of the U.S. Secretary of the Treasury), was largely responsible for initiating this policy change. He was a member of the upper income class that had taken a financial beating both during and immediately after World War I as inflation greatly reduced the real value of both government and corporate bonds. The lending class was very interested in reestablishing their wealth, which could be accomplished if the price level were returned to the value that existed before the war. The (incorrect) view at the time was that returning the British pound to its prewar gold parity ratio would accomplish this goal. In addition, the British also saw a return to the prewar parity as a move to help their country reestablish its financial leadership in the world. Many saw Britain's position falling relative to the United States, and there was real fear that if Britain did not go back on the gold standard soon, then the rest of the empire (Canada, Australia, and so on) would without Britain, resulting in a gold standard based not on the pound but on the U.S. dollar. Amazingly, this return to the prewar gold parity, "one of the worst monetary mistakes of the twentieth century" (Rolfe and Burtle 1973, 29), had strong public support. It was backed by the entire spectrum of major political parties in Britain and had the support of U.S. government officials as well.[3]

The problem was not that Britain had returned to the gold standard, but that it had done so at the prewar parity ratio. The prewar parity ratio implied an exchange rate between the U.S. dollar and the British pound of $4.86/pound. At the time the new policy was announced (April 28, 1925) the exchange rate was about 10 percent below the prewar parity ratio. In other words, in one fell swoop Churchill's policy caused the pound to be overvalued by about 10 percent relative to other currencies, most importantly the U.S. dollar and the French franc. That the pound was overvalued by 10 percent means that British goods and services were overpriced by about 10 percent on world markets. This was especially important for industries that depended heavily on international trade. In fact, five industries that had been very important to Britain's success during the 1800s, namely coal, cotton, wool textiles, shipbuilding, and iron and steel, were all greatly harmed by the overvaluation of the pound. In addition, the coal industry was also adversely affected by a major increase in German coal production after the French army evacuated the Ruhr region of Germany in 1924.[4] The problems in the British coal industry were so serious that the coal operators locked out the workers for seven months in an effort to force down wages. This coal strike eventually led to a nine-day nationwide general strike. The shipbuilding industry was adversely affected by technological advancements by Scandinavian shipbuilders (Kindleberger 1986, 17). Textiles were seriously impacted by competition from Japan and India. The problems in the coal, cotton and wool textiles, shipbuilding, and iron and steel industries were so severe that these industries accounted for half of all Britain's insured unemployment by 1929. This fact helps explain why the unemployment rates shown in table 4.1 stayed high during the latter half of the 1920s. In addition, since some of these five industries tended to be concentrated in particular regions of the country (for example, coal in Wales), enormous disparities developed among regional unemployment rates. For example, in 1923 the unemployment rate in Wales was 6.4 percent and in London, 10.1 percent. By 1929 the unemployment rate in Wales was 19.3 percent, while in London it was 5.6 percent (Garside 1990, 10). Given the reluctance of Britain's citizens to move around the country in search of work, these regional pockets of unemployment persisted over time and kept the aggregate unemployment rate high.

Britain's economic problems were exacerbated by the behavior of monetary authorities in both the United States and France. While the pound was the major overvalued currency, the dollar and franc were the major undervalued currencies, so the balance-of-payments deficit experienced by the United Kingdom was against surpluses in the United States and France. Therefore, gold flowed from Britain to the United States and France. Under the gold standard, that gold inflow should have been monetized, that is, both the United States and France should have experienced monetary expansions. These monetary expansions would have raised prices in both countries, which would have made British goods more competitive relative to U.S. and French goods. In this way, Britain would move toward balance in its international accounts.

However, this process did not occur. Neither the U.S. nor the French money supplies rose by amounts consistent with the quantity of gold flowing into those countries. The United States broke the rules of the gold standard and chose to sterilize their gold inflow. France accumulated major amounts of gold, which raised their gold reserve backing their money supply from 40.45 percent in June 1928 to over 60 percent by the end of 1931.[5] As a result, from 1925 to 1929 the United States experienced a mild deflation, and in France, from the 1926 franc stabilization through to 1929, the price level fell slightly (Temin 1989, 5). Since U.S. and French prices did not rise, the British bore the brunt of adjustment with restrictive monetary policies and accompanying slow economic growth. Thus, during the last half of the 1920s Britain's economy grew slowly relative to the other countries. In fact, using industrial production as a measure, the only major industrial country that Britain outperformed from 1925 to 1929 was Italy (Rolf and Burtle 1973, 20).

By 1927 the British were quite concerned about the balance-of-payments deficits and lack of monetary expansion in the surplus countries. In an effort to persuade the United States to allow monetary expansion to take place, Montague Norman, head of the Bank of England, traveled to the United States to meet with representatives of the central banks of the United States, Germany, and France. The Federal Reserve was represented by Benjamin Strong, Governor of the Federal Reserve Bank of New York.[6] They met on Long Island, New York, at the residence of then–Secretary of the Treasury Ogden Mills. According to Kindleberger, the purpose of the conference was to decide the best way to relieve the British balance-of-payments deficit: whether to reduce U.S. interest rates or raise them in Britain (1986, 50). Apparently very little was recorded about the decisions made at the conference except that the Federal Reserve agreed to lower interest rates in the United States in an effort to stem the gold inflow from Britain. An additional factor in the Federal Reserve's decision was the fact that the United States was in the midst of a mild recession at the time. The Federal Reserve reduced the discount rate by a half point and purchased $230 million worth of government securities (Eastburn 1965, 69).

This action by the Federal Reserve had two effects. First, it helped slow the gold flow from Britain to the United States, although this turned out to be only temporary. During 1927, $30.8 million worth of gold flowed from Britain to the United States, then it dropped to $5.0 million during 1928 (Federal Reserve Board of Governors 1943, 540). The second effect had more important implications: the monetary expansion of 1927 is considered by many economists to be an important factor in setting off the U.S. stock market advance of the late 1920s.[7] Easy credit conditions often show up early in the form of higher equity prices, and this appears to have been the case in 1927.

British economic growth improved in 1927, but slowed again in 1928. The consensus view holds that the British growth slowdown both indirectly and directly emanated from the United States. The indirect result occurred because of reduced U.S. lending abroad. As the New York stock exchange boomed, American investors reduced their foreign lending and instead placed their funds in U.S. equities. This reduction in foreign lending had adverse affects on countries that were dependent upon this capital inflow, which included Germany (see the following discussion) as well as countries dependent upon exports of primary products (that is, commodities). These commodity-exporting countries included several countries in Latin America as well as in Asia and Oceania (Kindleberger 1986, 55–56). The loss of the capital inflow placed these countries in deficit positions in their balance of payments, which necessitated restrictive monetary policies. These commodity-exporting countries accounted for a large proportion of Britain's exports, and as they experienced slow growth, their imports from Britain fell (Kirby 1981, 57–58). In this way, British exports were adversely affected by the severe slowdown in U.S. foreign lending.

Britain was also directly affected by events in the United States. When the U.S. growth slowdown began in 1929, U.S. imports diminished from all countries including Britain. This reduction in British exports caused the British current account to deteriorate, which increased their balance-of-payments deficit with the United States. As a result, during 1929 over $41 million worth of gold flowed from Britain to the United States. The resulting tight monetary policy in Britain placed upward pressure on interest rates, and that, combined with the slowdown in exports, plunged the country into recession.[8]

4.2. Germany

We gaze at [the American soldiers] in silence. They stand about us in a semicircle, fine, powerful fellows; clearly they have always had plenty to eat . . .

They are wearing new uniforms and greatcoats; their boots are water-tight and fit well; their rifles are good and their pouches full of ammunition. They are all fresh and unused.

Compared to these fellows we [German soldiers] are a perfect band of robbers. Our uniforms are bleached with the mud of years, with the rains of the Argonne, the chalk of Champagne, the bog waters of Flanders; our greatcoats ragged and torn by barbed wire, shell splinters and shrapnel, cobbled with crude stitches, stiff with clay and in some instances even with blood; our boots broken, our rifles weary, our ammunition almost at an end; we are all of us dirty, all alike gone to wrack, all weary. The war has passed over us like a steam roller.

—*Erich Maria Remarque (1931, 27–28)*

4.2.1. War and Reparations

World War I had extremely adverse affects on both the German people and the German economy. During the war (1914–18), Germany suffered 1,773,700 soldiers killed by battle casualties and disease. This figure represents about 2.6 percent of the country's population at that time. In addition, an estimated 763,000 German civilians died of starvation and diseases associated with malnutrition as a result of severe food shortages caused by the embargo. Another 150,000 German civilians died of the flu.

The war was also associated with a significant reduction in economic output. Here is the index of industrial production for 1913 through 1923 (taken from Petzina 1990, 6):

Year	Index (1928 = 100)
1913	98
1914	81
1915	66
1916	63
1917	61
1918	56
1919	37
1920	54
1921	65
1922	70
1923	46

The economy bottomed out in 1919 because even though hostilities were over, the blockade remained in effect until July 1919. Output was about 62 percent lower in 1919 than in 1913. In addition, 1919 agricultural output was about 55 to 60 percent below the 1913 level. While output was at such low levels, roughly 10 million soldiers returned home along with an additional million recently freed prisoners of war, many seeking work (Braun 1990, 34). Large-scale unemployment resulted.

The Armistice of November 1918 and the Treaty of Versailles, signed in 1919, imposed terms on the Germans that many at the time considered quite harsh. The German leaders had little choice, however, since widespread mutiny and desertion among soldiers and sailors had left them with little military power. Germany was forced to cede about 13 percent of its prewar territory on which about 10 percent of the country's population lived. The ceded land represented 14.6 percent of Germany's arable land prior to the war, and it held 74.5 percent of the country's iron ore deposits, 68.1 percent of its zinc ore, and 26 percent of its coal deposits (Stolper 1940, 136).

To many observers the harshest terms were the reparations Germany agreed to pay to the victors. The treaty specified initial amounts: Germany was required to hand over a significant proportion of its shipping fleet and railroad rolling stock, vast amounts of coal, and military hardware, as well as foreign exchange and government bonds. The total amount of reparations due was to be determined by the Allied Reparations Commission, which finally decided on an amount in April 1921. Germany was to pay the sum of 132 billion gold marks (about $33 billion) of which 8.0 billion gold marks were credited for the payments already made (Kindleberger 1986, 19). With interest compounded, the annual payments to meet this obligation were estimated to be about 10 percent of Germany's net national product.[9]

Just after the war ended many warned against imposing terms on Germany that were too harsh. One famous figure sounding alarms was the brilliant British economist John Maynard Keynes, who discussed the potential ramifications of imposing terms beyond Germany's ability to pay.

————➤•○•◄————

If we take the view that for at least a generation to come Germany cannot be trusted with even a modicum of prosperity, that while all our recent Allies are angels of light, all our recent enemies, Germans, Austrians, Hungarians, and the rest, are children of the devil, that year by year Germany must be kept impoverished and her children must be ringed round by enemies . . . then heaven help us all. If we aim deliberately at the impoverishment of Central Europe, vengeance, I dare predict, will not limp. Nothing can then delay for very long that final civil war between the forces of Reaction and the despairing convulsions of Revolution, before which the horrors of the late German war will fade into nothing, and which will destroy, whoever is victor, the civilisation and the progress of our generation.

—*John Maynard Keynes (1919, 28)*

————➤•○•◄————

4.2.2. Budget Deficits

During the war Germany experienced extremely large government budget deficits, and the reparations payments imposed after the war certainly did not help the situation. The budget deficits appeared during the war because taxes were never raised in any meaningful way to help cover the expenses incurred. When the war broke out the widespread expectation was that it would be quite short and therefore inexpensive. After all, the German army fully expected to march straight to Paris and present terms of surrender to the French. The Germans were badly mistaken, of course, because a few short months after moving into southern Belgium and northern France the German army found itself dug into trenches facing the British and French armies in their own trenches. Both sides remained there for nearly four years, killing each other's soldiers at an appalling rate. Meanwhile, the German army was also fighting an all-out war against the Russians on the eastern front. Thus, the war was far more expensive than the German government, or anyone else for that matter, ever imagined. The decision not to raise taxes significantly at the outset, or in any significant amount thereafter, meant that large budget deficits would be incurred. The deficits as a percent of net national product were, in fact, huge:

Year	Budget Deficit (as % of NNP)
1914	15.9
1915	52.1
1916	79.6
1917	62.3
1918	41.8
1919	33.9
1920	19.0
1921	10.2
1922	6.2
1923	17.2

Source: Sommariva and Tullio (1987, 123, 125)

The central bank, the Reichsbank, bought a large proportion of these bonds and printed the money to do so.[10] As a result, the monetary growth rate became quite rapid during the war, which resulted in incredibly high inflation rates by the early 1920s.[11] To see how the rapid monetary growth generated inflation, we take a brief detour to discuss the relationship between money and prices.

An Aside on the Equation of Exchange

The relationship between monetary growth and prices can be seen through Irving Fisher's equation of exchange:

$$M V = P Y$$

where M is the stock of money, V is the velocity of money, P is the price level, and Y is output. The left-hand side of the equation represents nominal aggregate demand: the stock of money is the number of units of money (for example, dollars, marks, or whatever) in circulation, and velocity measures the average number of times per period that each unit of money is used to buy final goods and services. When we multiply the stock of money times the average number of times each unit is spent on final goods and services, the result is the volume of total spending on final goods and services, or aggregate demand in nominal terms.

On the right-hand side of the equation, P is the price level and Y is output. The product of the two is nominal income, or aggregate supply in nominal terms. Setting the left-hand side equal to the right-hand side imposes the equilibrium condition that aggregate demand equals aggregate supply.

It is useful to put the equation of exchange in percent change form:

$$DM + DV = DP + DY$$

where DM represents the monetary growth rate, DV is velocity growth, DP is the inflation rate, and DY is output growth. The effects of changes in monetary growth on output and prices critically depend on the behavior of velocity, which reflects the demand for money. Suppose, for example, that total spending had been constant with both monetary growth and velocity growth at zero percent. Now, let the monetary growth rate rise to five percent and stay there. A number of possible scenarios exist. First, we might choose to simply hold all of the newly printed money, take it home and hide it in cookie jars or stuff it in mattresses. If we did this, there would be no change in total spending because velocity falls by five percent, which keeps the left-hand side of the equation constant.

Another possibility is that we choose to hold some, but not all, of the new money and spend the rest. In this case, total spending would rise because velocity falls but by less than five percent. Yet another possibility is that we spend all of the new money on goods and services. Here, total spending would rise by five percent because we hold none of the new money. In this case, velocity remains constant, that is, its growth rate remains at zero. Finally, we might spend not only the five percent of new money balances, but some additional money we are holding as well. In this case total spending rises by more than five percent because velocity rises.

In order to decide which scenario is likely to occur, it is important to understand that velocity's behavior depends on the attractiveness of holding money. If a rise in the monetary growth rate makes money more attractive to hold, then we will choose to hold some of the new money as opposed to spending it, so velocity would fall. If the rise in monetary growth makes money less attractive to hold, then we would spend not only the newly created money but some of our existing holdings as well. In this case velocity would rise. Therefore, if something happens to make money more attractive to hold, velocity falls. If money becomes less attractive to hold, velocity rises.

Historically, a very important determinant of the public's desire to hold money has been the expected change in the price level. Since money has a fixed nominal value, its real value varies inversely with the price level. If the price level falls, a given quantity of nominal money balances has more purchasing power. Conversely, if the price level rises, a given quantity of nominal money balances has less purchasing power.

What matters is not so much what the price level has done, but what the public *expects* it to do. After all, if you were caught holding a given stock of nominal money balances while the price level unexpectedly rose, there would be no point in getting rid of the money because that would not get the lost value back. But *if you expected the price level to keep on rising,* then you would expect further losses and have a strong incentive to get rid of your money holdings. On the other hand, if you expected the price level to fall, you would have a strong incentive to hang on to the money and even acquire more because you would expect the real value of money holdings to rise. Therefore, if the public expects the price level to go up, velocity will rise because money becomes less attractive to hold as an asset. Conversely, if the public expects the price level to fall, velocity will fall because money becomes more attractive to hold as an asset.[12]

4.2.3.   The German Hyperinflation

Table 4.2 presents Fisher's equation of exchange in growth rates for Germany from 1914 to 1923.[13] During the war years (1914–18), the rapid monetary growth did not result in especially high inflation rates for two main reasons: (1) a system of wage and price controls was in place, and (2) velocity was falling, which tells us that the public was willing to hold a good proportion of the newly created money. Sommariva and Tullio (1987) argue that although the German mark was depreciating by about 5.7 percent per year during the war, the public expected the mark to return to its prewar value when the war ended. Since the public expected the value of the mark to rise in the future, they were willing to hold additional money balances. You can see, however, that the public clearly revised their expectations in 1919. Velocity, which had been falling for five consecutive years, suddenly began to rise very rapidly. This pattern suggests that after the war the public realized that inflation, which suggested further depreciation of the mark, was the order of the day and that the mark would not be returning to its prewar value. As a result, the public's demand for money fell sharply and spending rose significantly. The inflation rate rose dramatically as a result.

TABLE 4.2.   Monetary Growth, Velocity Growth, Inflation, and Output Growth, Germany, 1914–23 (in percentages)

Year	DM	DV	DP	DY
1914	16.1	−5.7	30.2	−19.8
1915	26.6	−18.5	18.4	−10.3
1916	17.0	−22.0	2.0	−7.0
1917	42.4	−10.9	34.4	−2.9
1918	53.2	−34.0	20.7	−1.5
1919	80.3	129.2	227.7	−18.2
1920	65.4	32.2	79.3	18.2
1921	33.8	118.6	142.4	10.1
1922	287.8	3,847.1	4,125.8	9.2
1923	2.13×10^8	8.53×10^{10}	8.55×10^{10}	−27.1

Source: Data for DM is from Sommariva and Tullio 1987, 124, 126; data for DP taken from Sargent 1986, 80–81; data for DY taken from Cagan 1956, 105.

Note: DM = monetary growth rate, proxied by currency growth rate.
DV = velocity growth, computed as DV = (DP + DY) – DM.
DP = inflation rate, percent change in the wholesale price index.
DY = output growth, computed as percent change in output.
DM + DV = DP + DY

The hyperinflation occurred in 1922 and 1923. As table 4.2 shows, the high inflation during 1922 was due more to rapid velocity growth than to monetary growth as the public was spending their cash balances at very rapid rates. In 1923, however, monetary growth was as responsible as velocity growth. The printing presses were running at full tilt; according to Braun, "at the end of 1923 more than 300 paper mills and about 2,000 printing presses worked continuously to supply the public with *Reichsbank* notes" (1990, 39). People required boxes and carts to haul around the paper money required for everyday transactions. The transactions costs of using these huge quantities of currency became so high that "often there was a return to primitive barter trade: four eggs for a hair cut, two briquettes for admission to the cinema, forty eggs for a burial (first class with sermon)" (39). The hyperinflation had devastating effects on household savings. "A bank account of 60,000 marks, the interest from which would, in 1913, have enabled one to lead a comfortable life in retirement, would not buy a daily newspaper in April 1923" (40).

With the situation completely out of hand by summer 1923, the Reichsbank took a series of steps to try to stop the hyperinflation. In August, they told the government that they would no longer provide unlimited financing of the government deficit and that effective November 16 they would no longer rediscount government bills.[14] In mid-October the Rentenbank was established, which would take over the note-issuing function of the Reichsbank. The Rentenbank would issue notes in a new unit of account, the rentenmark. One rentenmark was worth one trillion (10^{12}) marks. Later, the reichsmark was introduced, with one reichsmark worth one rentenmark. The purpose of introducing the new units of account was simply to reduce the number of paper notes needed for transactions. The Rentenbank had binding limits on how many rentenmarks they would issue: 3.2 billion; of which 1.2 billion could be provided to the government. In December 1923 the government challenged the Rentenbank on the currency limitations, but the bank stood by its limits (Sargent 1986, 84).

Currency in circulation peaked in mid-November when the policy of no longer rediscounting government bills took effect. The public apparently considered the new anti-inflation policy to be a credible one and was willing to hold currency again. This, combined with the huge reduction in monetary growth, resulted in an inflation rate during 1924 of just 12.0 percent (Sargent 1986, 81).

4.2.4. Recovery and Recession

The Dawes Plan was the name given to the efforts of an international commission charged to improve Germany's financial condition. The commission was chaired by an American named Charles Dawes.[15] The Dawes Plan stipulated that, starting in 1924–25, Germany was to make annual reparations payments of 1.0 billion reichsmarks plus an amount determined by a "prosperity index" that was based on consumption of a wide variety of items. Payments would rise over time and peak in 1929 at 3.0 billion reichsmarks. This new payment schedule represented a deferral of Germany's reparations obligation, reducing immediate debt service payments to a fraction of what had been stipulated earlier. In addition, a loan was made to Germany, financed by bond sales in several countries. The loan was 800 million reichsmarks worth of foreign currency. Half the funds were raised in the United States.

The payment rescheduling and loan were very important because the combination of the two gave the German government short-term relief. This was critical in 1924 because there were genuine concerns that the economy would slide again and that hyperinflation would return. Eichengreen notes that in the spring of 1924 nominal interest rates were 44 percent, which, given the relatively low inflation at that time, translates into real interest rates of over 30 percent (1992b, 150). These very high real rates simply reflect the risk and uncertainty that inflation might return. Three months after the loan, nominal interest rates had fallen to 11 percent. The loan was also important because it was followed by a wave of additional foreign lending to Germany, especially from the United States. Attracted by the relatively high German interest rates, Americans were lending around $500 million per year to Europe from 1924 to 1928, with much of that total going to Germany. Total U.S. lending to Europe was $2.9 billion from 1924 to 1929.

The German economy made a remarkable recovery. Per-capita production more than doubled from 1923 to 1927, with prewar output levels achieved by 1925 (Sargent 1986, 95). In addition, labor fared well because high levels of investment spending generated significant productivity gains that resulted in rapid rises in real wages. By the late 1920s the average German was much better off economically than before World War I.

Unfortunately, it all started to go sour in the latter half of 1928. The heavy U.S. lending during the 1920s had fueled the investment boom:

according to Lewis, during 1927 and 1928 net investment was 11.8 percent of national income, with half the total funded from abroad (1949, 41). Moreover, 40 percent of this lending was short term, meaning that those funds could get pulled out on fairly short notice. This is exactly what happened. By late 1928 the huge gains in U.S. stock prices made equities look very attractive to U.S. lenders. They chose to reduce their lending to German institutions and instead placed their funds in U.S. stocks. During the first half of 1928, Americans bought $200 million in new capital issues in Germany. During the second half of the year, they bought just $76.6 million (Kindleberger 1986, 55). Lending during 1929 was down even further.

The fall in foreign lending to Germany placed the Reichsbank in a difficult position. Worried that the lending decline might turn into a major capital outflow, they restricted monetary growth and pushed interest rates up. In doing that, they generated monetary policies "more severe than those undertaken by the Federal Reserve in 1928" (Temin 1989, 24). As a result, the investment spending boom came to an abrupt halt, and the German economy started to grow much more slowly. The slow growth turned into a full-blown recession by mid-1929.[16]

4.3. France

To be sure, the French retained an enormous respect for Germany's power and her potential for recovery. But respect was coupled with simple hatred, not with wisdom. Nothing so clearly demonstrates the brutal milieu of postwar Europe . . . as the unforgiving—and unforgivable—remark of [French Prime Minister] Clemenceau . . . "there are twenty million Germans too many."

—*C. Paul Vincent (1985, 85)*

4.3.1.   Rebuilding and the Franc Crisis

Fighting World War I was a very costly exercise for France as well. An estimated 1.4 million French soldiers died of battle wounds and disease, which represented about 3.5 percent of the population at the time. In addition, a great deal of the actual fighting on the western front took place on French soil, in the northern section of the country where much of the industrial production was located. During most of the period of hostilities, the German army occupied 8.0 percent of France's territory that before the war had accounted for over 30 percent of the country's prewar industrial production, "including most of its coal, iron, steel and copper industries" (Moure 1991, 11). The German army deliberately destroyed much of this productive capacity during their retreat in 1918. In 1919, France's industrial production was just over half of what it had been in 1913. During the same six years the wholesale price level had risen about 350 percent.

So the "victory" had provided France with a diminished population, lower living standards, and an economy in ruins. A major rebuilding effort had to be made, and the French quickly went to work. The government made compensation payments to private industry and, along with liquid assets built up during the war, these funds were used to purchase investment goods. As a result, the capital stock was upgraded to embody the newest technology. In addition, the government funded the rebuilding of public infrastructure. The funds for this rebuilding effort were borrowed: the government issued short-term debt and also borrowed from the Bank of France. The expectation was that this debt would be paid off in the near future when the Germans started making the reparations payments.

The reparations payments actually made were slow in coming and never covered the rebuilding costs. Meanwhile, the politicians could not agree on a tax hike. So France ended up monetizing the public debt that was being issued. The result was rapid monetary growth, rising inflation, and a major depreciation of the franc. By 1924 the situation was so serious that the politicians finally agreed on a tax increase that would balance the budget. Financial stability resulted and with it the end of what Eichengreen calls the "first phase of the crisis" (1992b, 173).

The second phase of the crisis began shortly thereafter. The tax hike was a particular burden on the working class and owners of small businesses. They responded at the ballot box by voting out the conservatives who were responsible for the tax hike and replacing them with leftists who wanted to use the tax system to redistribute income and wealth from the upper classes to the lower classes. A dispute over taxation broke out that lasted nearly two years. During this period, the country went through "ten different ministers of finance in almost as many governments" (Kindleberger 1986, 33). Meanwhile, the prospect of major taxes on income and wealth led the upper classes to move their financial capital out of the country. This capital outflow, along with a general crisis of confidence about France's ability to solve its fiscal problems, led to a major depreciation of the franc. At the same time inflation was getting out of control. The upper classes were unwilling to purchase public debt, so the Bank of France ended up buying it. The resulting money creation generated an inflation rate of 350 percent from June to July 1926. The franc–pound exchange rate went from 90 per pound in 1925 to 240 per pound in July 1926. Against the U.S. dollar, the franc fell in value from 5.4 francs per dollar at the start of 1925 to 49 per dollar on July 21, 1926 (Eichengreen 1992b, 183).

4.3.2. Stabilization

The French finally stabilized the situation in July 1926. A dispute had broken out among the leftist politicians, and some broke ranks and backed financial stabilization. With the help of these politicians, Raymond Poincaré was made prime minister. He had the support of the upper classes because it was well known that he opposed taxes on income and wealth. He served as his own finance minister and was granted full powers by Parliament to make fiscal changes. His first move was to lower taxes, which very quickly reversed the capital outflow. Within a week, the franc appreciated from 240 per pound to 190 per pound. Once the capital outflow was reversed, he raised indirect taxes (for example, sales and excise taxes) and cut spending to get the budget deficit under control. The effects of these policies were remarkable.[17] By December the exchange rates were 124 francs per pound and 25.51 francs per dollar. At that point the franc was pegged by the Bank of France.

These new exchange rates were made official in June 1928 when France returned to the gold standard. Unfortunately, it turned out that at these exchange rates the franc was undervalued, about 25 percent according to an estimate cited by Hamilton (1987, 146). As a result, France experienced a major gold inflow with much of it coming from Britain and the United States. France's gold reserves increased from 29 to 82 billion francs from 1928 to 1932. Yet over the same period the Bank of France's note circulation increased by only 22 billion francs (Moure 1991, 46). In other words, the Bank of France was sterilizing a large proportion of the gold inflow. This placed the burden of adjustment on the deficit country, in this case Britain, which ran balance-of-payments deficits every year from 1927 to 1931 except for a small surplus in 1928. The United States was also a deficit country, at least with respect to France. While the United States ran overall balance-of-payments surpluses each year during the 1920s, it ran sizable deficits with France starting in 1928. From 1928 to 1932 the United States experienced a net gold outflow to France of over $1.2 billion (Board of Governors of the Federal Reserve 1943, 540). In 1928 alone, over $307 million worth of U.S. gold flowed to France. Hamilton cites this gold outflow to France as one of the reasons (along with the stock market advance) that the Federal Reserve instituted the monetary tightening in early 1928 that eventually initiated the Great Depression (1987, 147).

CHAPTER 5

The Start of the
Great Depression, 1929–30

5.1. Monetary Policy and the Stock Market

—————⇒»·0·«⇐—————

The period 1929–33 began as a cyclical contraction much like others, this time in response to the immoderate concern of the Federal Reserve Board about speculation in the stock market.
                                            —Anna J. Schwartz (1981, 25)

By eleven o'clock the market had degenerated into a wild, mad scramble to sell . . . [while] outside the Exchange in Broad Street a weird roar could be heard.
                    —John Kenneth Galbraith describing events at the
                    New York Stock Exchange on Black Thursday,
                    October 24, 1929 (1954, 99)

—————⇒»·0·«⇐—————

The widespread belief among economists who have studied the Great Depression is that the cause of the initial downturn in the United States was the tight monetary policy that the Federal Reserve began in early 1928. This policy was carried out largely for one reason: to stem the rapid advance in stock prices. Officials at the Federal Reserve were convinced that a speculative frenzy was taking place on Wall Street, and they were especially concerned about member banks' role in providing the fuel by lending for stock market speculation.

From January 1928 to May 1929 the Federal Reserve took a series of actions designed to tighten credit conditions. They sold $405 million worth of government securities, raised the discount rate in three stages from 3.5 percent to 5.0 percent, raised the buying rate on bankers' acceptances, and engaged in moral suasion in which they jawboned member banks to stop making speculative securities loans (Eastburn 1965, 69). It was indeed a tight monetary policy. Hamilton notes that "in terms of magnitudes consciously controlled by the Fed, it would be difficult to design a more contractionary policy than that initiated in January 1928; the Fed had virtually no more securities to sell nor balances of acceptances to be reduced" (1987, 147).

What potentially could have been an extremely contractionary policy turned out, in fact, to be only mildly contractionary. If bank borrowing from the Federal Reserve had remained unchanged, the monetary base would have fallen by $889 million, or 12.0 percent of its total, over just the seven-month period from December 1927 to July 1928 (Hamilton 1987, 148). This decline would have occurred because of a gold outflow, the sale of U.S. government securities by the Federal Reserve, and reduction of bills of acceptances held by the Federal Reserve. Yet the monetary base declined by only 1.2 percent during 1928, in large part because there was an enormous increase in member bank borrowing from the Federal Reserve. This borrowing alone offset more than half of the contraction in the base caused by the other factors.

Banks were eager to borrow from the Federal Reserve because they could borrow at 5.0 percent, the discount rate at the time, and then turn around and lend out the funds at rates even higher. Even though the discount rate had been increased from 3.5 percent to 5.0 percent, money market interest rates had gone up even more. According to Hamilton, money market rates had risen sharply for two reasons: rising demand for money associated with increased trading volume in the stock market and increased demand for credit for the purpose of purchasing stocks (1987, 149).

The effects of the tight monetary policy and the rising demand for money are shown in figure 5.1, which plots yields on long- and short-term U.S. Treasury securities. A familiar pattern is shown: the tight monetary policy raised short-term interest rates above long-term rates for several months. As a result, the yield curve, which is the plot of yields on bonds of different maturities but of equal risk, took on a downward slope.[1]

However, the tight monetary policy took time to have contractionary effects on aggregate economic activity. Restrictive credit conditions usu-

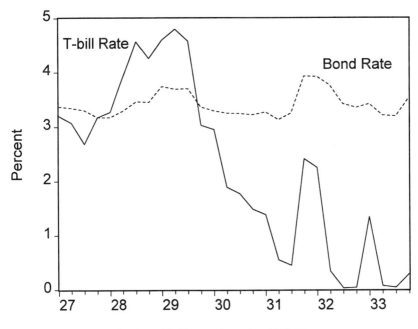

Fig. 5.1.   Yield curve inversion, 1928–29

ally show up first in the sectors of the economy most sensitive to monetary restriction: consumer durables and investment spending. According
to R. A. Gordon, residential construction had been falling since its peak
in early 1928. Excess capacity developed in the auto and tire industries
by late 1928, and overall spending on consumer durables peaked in the
first quarter of 1929 (1961, 426). The index of industrial production
peaked in the spring of 1929. According to the National Bureau of Economic Research, the peak in aggregate economic activity occurred in
August 1929.

Therefore, the Great Depression began in August 1929 when the economic growth slowdown turned into an actual decline in economic output. During the early stages of the recession, output was falling quite
rapidly, although nothing like what was to come later. Friedman and
Schwartz report that "during the two months from the cyclical peak in
August 1929 to the [stock market] crash [in October], production,
wholesale prices, and personal income fell at annual rates of 20 percent,
13½ percent, and 17 percent respectively" (1963, 306).

While the stock market crash is usually identified as occurring in
October, stock prices actually peaked on September 3 when the *New*

York Times index of industrial stocks stood at 452.[2] The combination of tight credit conditions and the recession moved the index down to 403 on October 24 (Black Thursday). The panic occurred on Monday and Tuesday, October 28 and 29, when prices fell by a total of 23 percent. A brief rally followed, but then prices fell again. The bottom for 1929 was reached on November 13 when the *New York Times* index hit 224. Stock prices had fallen about 50 percent from their peak in September.

There are at least three reasons why the stock market crash caused an accelerated decline in economic output. First, the decline in stock values (about $20 billion) reduced household wealth, which is consistent with falling consumption expenditures. Second, the decline in stock prices reduced the market value of existing capital relative to new capital goods, which reduces the demand for new plant and machinery.[3] Third, and potentially most important, is the increase in uncertainty generated by the crash. An increase in uncertainty about the economic future would have two effects: a rise in the precautionary demand for money that puts upward pressure on interest rates and lowers the velocity of money, and further reductions in household consumption expenditures, especially on durable goods because they tend to be big-ticket items.[4] Purchases of durable goods can also often be delayed.

Whatever the channels by which the crash affected the economy, the recession clearly worsened after October. To illustrate, here is the Federal Reserve's adjusted index of industrial production of manufacturers for the latter months of 1929:

Month	*Index (1923–25 = 100)*
August	122
September	121
October	119
November	110
December	101

Source: Federal Reserve Board of Governors, *Federal Reserve Bulletin* (May 1933, 286)

While the stock market crash appears to have accelerated the rate of economic decline, the crash was not associated with bank panics as had occurred so often before in the United States. In the opinion of Friedman and Schwartz, this was because effective policies were carried out by the Federal Reserve Bank of New York (1963, 334–39). Initiated by the bank's governor, George Harrison, the New York Fed during the week of the stock market crash lent an additional $130 million to district member banks and purchased $160 million worth of government securities. In this way, an enormous amount of liquidity was provided to the financial system. Friedman and Schwartz summarize the effort by saying that "the actions taken by the New York Reserve Bank were timely and effective. Despite the stock market crash, there were no panic increases in money market rates such as those in past market crises, and no indirect effects on confidence in banks which might have arisen if there had been any sizable defaults on security loans" (1963, 339).

Unfortunately, these timely actions of the Federal Reserve Bank of New York were criticized by the Federal Reserve Board in Washington. The point of contention was the purchase of $160 million worth of government securities. This exceeded the amount the New York Fed was authorized to purchase. They had simply done it on their own because it was obvious to Harrison and the New York bank directors that such action was necessary to keep the crash from spreading. While the board in Washington later approved the purchase ex post, they made it clear to the New York Fed that such actions should not occur again. This reining in of the New York Fed turned out to be important to events later on. When the Depression deepened, officials at the New York Fed talked about the proper actions they felt should be carried out, but never again did they have the courage to take actions without the board's approval.

5.2. 1930

The world has been slow to realise that we are living this year in the shadow of one of the greatest economic catastrophes of modern history.

—*John Maynard Keynes (1930, 135)*

1930 is arguably the most puzzling year of the Great Depression.
—*Christina Romer (1990, 599)*

While there is little disagreement that stringent monetary policy initiated the Great Depression and the stock market crash accelerated the decline in late 1929, there is some controversy as to why the Depression deepened to the extent that it did during 1930. One clear reason why output kept falling was the continuing decline in the stock of money. Friedman and Schwartz consider this factor very important and note that the monetary decline was severe; "from the cyclical peak in August 1929 . . . the money stock declined 2.6 percent to October 1930, a larger decline than during the whole of all but four preceding reference cycle contractions" (1963, 307–8).

Work by Temin (1976) and Gordon and Wilcox (1981) suggests that monetary stringency alone is not sufficient to explain the economy's behavior during 1930.[5] Gordon and Wilcox find this result by first estimating the relationship between money and nominal income from 1920.II to 1928.IV. Using the estimated parameters relating money to nominal income during the 1920s, they forecast nominal income during the 1930s using the actual values of the M2 measure of money that occurred during that period. The predicted values are estimates of what nominal income would have been if monetary factors alone had been responsible for the falling output and prices. They find that the predicted value of nominal income is above that of the actual value during the entire period of the Depression. During 1930, a big drop-off of actual income from predicted income occurs (Gordon and Wilcox 1981, 64). Based on these results, they conclude that the 1930 output decline was due in part to monetary stringency, but in addition some nonmonetary factors were at work as well.[6]

Before we investigate which nonmonetary factors were at work, it is useful to view the sources of the output decline in 1930. Here are the changes in the spending components from 1929 to 1930 in billions of 1972 dollars:[7]

GNP	−29.5
Consumption	−15.6
Investment	−12.2
Business Inventories	−5.1
Government Purchases	+3.7
Net Exports	−0.2

It is very unusual for consumption expenditures to account for over half the decline in output during a recession. It is far more often the case that investment accounts for the majority of the fall in spending (Hall 1990, 14–17). Therefore, a number of studies addressing the 1930 output decline focus on nonmonetary factors that might be responsible for the unusually sharp decline in consumption spending.

Several economists contend that the major nonmonetary factor at work during 1930 was the behavior of stock prices. After the 1929 crash, a "suckers' rally" followed from November 1929 to April 1930 when stock prices rose 18 percent. But then prices plunged again; from April 1930 to the end of the year the Standard and Poor's index of common stocks fell 50 percent. Temin believes the decline in equity prices changed people's expectations, although he discusses at length the problems with measuring the effect (1976). Romer contends that the stock price decline can explain all of the decline in consumption spending on durables that accounts for over 20 percent of the total decline in consumption spending during 1930 (1990). She notes that during 1930 output of consumer durable goods fell 32.4 percent, while output of perishable goods fell by only 1.6 percent. She points out that these numbers are consistent with an increase in uncertainty because durables are big-ticket items and their purchases can often be postponed. She argues that the stock market crash increased the degree of uncertainty about the economic future and cites forecasters of the day as evidence of this uncertainty. She presents statistical evidence suggesting that the crash had a great impact on spending on durables and a lesser impact on nondurables and semidurables expenditures that she argues would be less sensitive than durables to an increase in uncertainty. Based on her results, Romer concludes that "the negative effect of stock market variability is more than strong enough to account for the entire decline in real consumer spending on durables that occurred in late 1929 and 1930" (1990, 598–99).

Friedman and Schwartz also contend that the stock market crash was important. They note that the velocity of money fell 13 percent during 1930, a very sharp drop during just one year. Friedman and Schwartz argue that the rise in the demand for money is partly the result of the stock market crash, which raised the level of uncertainty and reduced spending (1963, 306–7). In the context of Friedman's money demand function, an increase in uncertainty raises the demand for money relative to alternative assets (1956). Since many sorts of consumer goods are among these alternative assets, the rise in uncertainty reduces consumption expenditures.

Other economists believe that price deflation during 1930 was more responsible for the deepening recession. The GNP deflator fell 3.3 percent during 1930 while the wholesale price index fell 15 percent. There are three reasons why this price deflation would cause the recession to worsen. First and foremost, since debt is specified in nominal terms instead of real purchasing power, falling prices raise the real burden of the debt. To illustrate, suppose you took out a loan with regular monthly payments that represent 10 percent of your monthly income. The dollar amount of the loan, or its nominal value, is fixed, as are the monthly payments. Now assume that the price level falls by 20 percent, implying that all prices fall by that proportion, including nominal wages. As a result, your nominal, or current dollar, income would fall by about 20 percent as well. Yet, because the debt is fixed in dollar terms, the 20 percent decline in the price level raises the real value of the debt by 20 percent. As a result, the debt payments that used to represent 10 percent of your income would now represent 12 percent (10 percent times 1.2) of your income, leaving you with less to spend on goods and services. This link between deflation, debt, and falling output was originally emphasized by Fisher (1933) and has received considerable backing in recent years as an influence in deepening the Depression, most notably by Mishkin (1978) and Kindleberger (1986). Mishkin argues that the increased burden of debt was an especially acute problem for households. He shows that from 1929 to 1930 real household liabilities rose 20 percent while real household asset holdings fell 4.0 percent, a deterioration that he calls "severe" (Mishkin 1978, 921). He shows that the 1929–30 increase in liabilities was three times the average annual increase for much of the post–World War II period.

In addition, during normal years the increase in liabilities (debt) was offset by increases in assets and net worth (savings and wealth). This situation was not the case during 1930; liabilities rose while assets, and thus the ability to pay back loans, fell. Many households went bankrupt as a result. Kindleberger notes that not just households but businesses with bank loans or outstanding bonds were also caught in the debt-deflation squeeze (1986).

This debt-deflation problem was particularly acute for farmers because prices received by farmers fell far more than the general price level.[8] While the GNP deflator was falling 3.3 percent from 1929 to 1930, prices of farm products fell 17.0 percent (Kindleberger 1986, 138). Since farmers typically held large mortgage debt, the real burden owed by farmers rose significantly during the early 1930s, and a great many farmers defaulted on their loans. In addition, farmers constituted a much larger proportion of the population during the 1930s than they do today; in 1930, 24.8 percent of Americans lived on farms, while in 1991 only 1.9 percent did (Council of Economic Advisors 1960 and 1993). Given the farm sector's importance in 1930, the widespread default by farmers during that period must have had significant contractionary effects on spending, employment, and production.

The second reason why deflation reduced spending is that, assuming the deflation was not anticipated, wealth was unexpectedly transferred from borrowers to lenders.[9] This transfer can have an impact on consumption expenditures by a channel known as the redistribution effect. Given nominal interest rates at the start of 1930—around 4.4 percent on high-grade corporate bonds—the deflation of 3.3 percent during the year implies that the borrower had to pay 7.7 percent in real terms over the course of the year, that is, interest of 4.4 percent plus an additional 3.3 percent because the real value of money required to make payments on the loans rose by that amount due to deflation. Meanwhile, the lender receives this 7.7 percent, 3.3 percent more than expected. Thus, borrowers ended up paying more, and the lenders receiving more, than would have been the case had the real value of money stayed level or the deflation been planned for. Since borrowers tend to have lower incomes than lenders, wealth was shifted from relatively poor households that spend a large proportion of their incomes on goods and services, to relatively wealthy households that spend a smaller proportion of their incomes on consumption. Downward pressure was placed on aggregate consumption expenditures as a result.

The third reason why deflation has a contractionary affect on spending is the expectations effect. This refers to the idea that the greater the deflation is and the longer it lasts, the more deflation in the future may be expected by households. If people expect prices to continue falling, they have an incentive to delay purchases, that is, to wait for further price declines before buying. This behavior results in a decline in current consumption spending.[10]

Another nonmonetary factor that some have suggested was partly responsible for the output decline of 1930 was the Smoot-Hawley Tariff Act. This act was passed by Congress in June 1930, although it passed the House of Representatives in 1929. Smoot-Hawley increased the tariff to a tax of over 50 percent on goods imported into the United States. It is important not just because it represented a major hike in U.S. tariff rates, but also because it prompted a retaliatory response from 60 other countries that raised their tariff rates as well. In fact, Smoot-Hawley has been described as "probably one of the most damaging pieces of legislation ever signed in the United States" (Council of Economic Advisors 1988, 147). In 1932 the League of Nations argued that Smoot-Hawley was partly responsible for the fall in commodity prices that was part of the worldwide deflation taking place at the time (1932, 65–66). Meltzer extends that argument by contending that Smoot-Hawley was a major force helping cause the output decline of the early 1930s (Meltzer 1976). He contends that the tariff and the retaliatory response to it caused a major reduction in U.S. exports and imports of agricultural and semifinished products, and with this big drop in demand for internationally traded products came a large fall in their prices. Thus, the price of goods traded internationally (for example, durables and commodities) fell relative to goods not traded internationally (for example, new houses). He goes on to argue that the resulting huge decline in agricultural prices was one reason why bank failures were so widespread in the U.S. Farm Belt.

Dornbusch and Fischer agree that Smoot-Hawley had a negative impact on U.S. output, but believe that the effect was relatively small (1986). They present two pieces of evidence to support their argument. First is that the 1922 Fordney-McCumber tariff raised rates by about the same order of magnitude that Smoot-Hawley did, but it was not followed by any major decline in output. Second, from 1929 to 1931 exports fell from 7 percent of GNP to 5.5 percent of GNP. Assuming a spending multiplier of two (which they consider an inflated estimate), Smoot-Hawley can explain an output decline of 3 percent, nowhere near the total that actually occurred over that same period.

Jones, in an exhaustive study of the tariff, discusses several cases where it clearly impacted trade (1934). For example, in retaliation against Smoot-Hawley, Swiss consumers boycotted U.S. products. Spain erected its own tariff wall, and U.S. auto sales to that country fell from 7,415 units in 1929 to 841 in 1931. However, it is not clear how much of that decline resulted from the influence of falling income upon trade rather than the tariff itself (Jones 1934, 61).

In sum, it is not completely clear why the economy contracted to the extent that it did during 1930. The monetary decline that helped initiate the recession in 1929 surely continued to have contractionary effects in 1930. However, this reduced monetary growth does not appear to have been of sufficient magnitude to completely explain the output drop during 1930. As a result, economists have searched for other factors to account for the deepening recession. The stock market crash, the deflationary pressures raising the burden of debt, and the Smoot-Hawley tariff are the leading candidates. The stock market reduced wealth and raised the degree of economic uncertainty, which increased the demand for money and caused households to reduce their purchases of consumer goods, especially durables. The deflation raised real debt burdens which resulted in bankruptcies and further declines in consumption expenditures. As for the Smoot-Hawley tariff, although the magnitude of its effect on the aggregate economy is not clear, it had some impact on U.S. exports and imports. Yet one thing is clear: as a result of these factors, the recession deepened during 1930.

CHAPTER 6

Sowing the
Seeds of Disaster

Every business man, banker and capitalist knows what it is and what it has done. It is the best financial system the world has ever seen. It has made this Nation and Government an impregnable force and the strongest the mind of man has devised.
—*John S. Williams, Comptroller of the Currency, in a public statement on the Federal Reserve Act (taken from Owen 1919, 104)*

The distinction between the initial economic downturn that began in 1929 and the free fall into the Great Depression of the 1930s has not always been made clear in the writings of economists about the Depression. Discussion has most often become focused upon looking for a *single* cause of the Depression. The several factors and the importance of the timing of these factors that contributed to the decline in the economy have rarely been put in clear context with each other. They have usually been treated as competing alternatives rather than what they were: coexisting and reinforcing factors in the plunge of the U.S. economy into the depths of the Great Depression. Often no distinction has been made in the timing of these factors and their effects upon the U.S. economy. After the start of the downturn in 1929, a deepening of the decline began in 1930. Then, a further steepening of the slide into unprecedented levels of unemployment developed in 1931 and 1932, and the low point was reached in 1933. And finally, the devastated U.S. economy staggered on through seemingly interminable pain and suffering until 1941.

At each stage of the decline there were new factors contributing to the changes: the stock market crash, the Smoot-Hawley tariff increase of 1930, unwise Federal Reserve policy throughout the decade, the very existence of the gold standard, the British end to the gold standard in 1931, the U.S. end to the gold standard in 1933, bank failures throughout the period, maintenance of high wages by the government, and the inaction of the Hoover administration from 1929 to 1932. Each had its impact upon events, but more importantly, the economy felt the impact of each factor at different points in time. It is necessary to keep this in mind because not only were some factors more important than others, some time periods were overwhelmingly more significant than others.

For example, as we saw in chapters 4 and 5, careful evaluation of the evidence has clearly supported those who have argued that the 1929 recession was initiated by changes in Federal Reserve monetary policy. The Federal Reserve's goal for this policy was to suppress what they saw as a speculative fever that had created the stock market advance of the late 1920s. The soaring stock market had been fueled by the rapid growth of bank credit, which allowed speculators to buy stock on margin and thus borrow most of the funds to buy shares in corporations. Therefore, in response the Federal Reserve reduced available credit and the money stock, and, in the process, it raised interest rates.

This tight monetary policy began in 1928. There seems little doubt that this was the dominant cause of the downturn in economic activity in the summer of 1929 and the stock market crash following in October of the same year. There also seems little reason to doubt that the fall in the stock market reinforced the movement of the economy toward a recession.

Milton Friedman and Anna Schwartz, in their *Monetary History of the United States 1867–1960* (1963), argue that as a result of these policies, the U.S. economy would certainly have experienced a very severe recession. However, they believe that something more needed to occur to make conditions bad enough to transform the situation into the Great Depression.

This chapter tries to address this issue by asking two important questions: (1) What transformed the economic decline of 1929–30 into a Great Depression lasting throughout the 1930s? and (2) Why was the Great Depression a worldwide event?

6.1. The Real Bills Doctrine

An act to provide for the establishment of the Federal reserve banks, to furnish an elastic currency, to afford a means of rediscounting commercial paper, to establish a more effective supervision of banking in the United States, and for other purposes.

—*Preamble to the Federal Reserve Act of 1913,
December 23, 1913 (ch. 6, vol. 38, 251, United States
Statutes at Large, 63d Congress 1913–1915)*

To understand how the economic decline of 1929–30 was transformed into the Great Depression, it is necessary to have some background in the operation of the financial system and especially the accepted role of the Federal Reserve system in the 1930s. It is even more important to develop an understanding of the principles that provided an economic basis for the formation of the Federal Reserve's policy.

The Federal Reserve in 1929 did not have either the coordinated power or the responsibilities it has today. It had been established in 1914 to help maintain the stability of our banking system. The Federal Reserve Act of 1913 was the law by which Congress set up the system and gave it the power and responsibility to lend to banks in times of financial crisis. This is a situation usually characterized by a disastrous shortage of liquidity in the banking system and by an inability of banks to pay depositors the money they demand. Liquidity is defined as assets easily and quickly converted to cash, in this case bank reserves. In the face of such a crisis, the Federal Reserve banks were to lend to, and thus provide liquidity to, individual banks.

However, a basic principle of the Federal Reserve's behavior was that these loans would not be made to banks that through poor management had found themselves on the edge of bankruptcy. Loans were to be made to banks that were *temporarily* short of liquid funds. To qualify, a bank should be perfectly sound and profitable, but faced with unexpectedly large withdrawals of cash. Such withdrawals were, and continue to be, a danger and problem inherent to the business of banking. Banks operate within an environment in which customers make deposits into accounts (checking accounts) that the banks promise to repay upon demand. Thus, they are called demand deposits. Therefore, banks can be thought to borrow funds from their depositors with the promise to repay them at any time the customer demands repayment. In addition, customers are promised interest on their deposits.

Here is the inherently risky part of banking. To pay this interest and make a profit as a thriving business, banks must lend out the funds deposited with them to others at a higher rate of interest than the banks pay their depositors. The way to do this is to make loans of longer maturity than the demand deposits. Because of the higher risks inherent with a long-term contract, longer maturity loans imply payment of a higher rate of interest. Bankers would say these loans are less liquid. Here lies the "fly in the ointment" of banking.

In order to make a profit, banks must borrow from their depositors with the promise to pay on demand and then lend to others for longer periods, that is, borrow short and lend long. Thus, their liabilities are more liquid than their assets. Bank loans need not be paid back on as short notice as bank depositors must be paid. This creates a situation in which banks effectively sell the benefits of liquidity to their depositors, and in the process they become illiquid themselves. This makes banking an inherently risky business, particularly in times of crisis.

Banks make bets that not all or even a large portion of their customers will demand payment (cash checks) all at once. When they lose this bet and there is a "run on the bank," a bank can not pay its depositors, in spite of the fact that the value of the bank's assets is perfectly adequate to match its liabilities. The result may well be forced bankruptcy (insolvency) for the bank because many of the bank's assets such as loans can not be sold quickly, or if they could would likely be sold at fire-sale prices. So in essence the bank's short-term liabilities exceed its short-term assets, and thus in the event of a bank run the ever-present illiquidity would be transformed into insolvency, bank closure, and financial loss to depositors and bank owners alike.

The principle by which sound and prudent bank behavior had been judged for over a hundred years had been the commercial loan theory. This standard required banks to concentrate their assets in short-term loans to businesses (less than one year in maturity). These loans were considered safe, relatively liquid, and "self-liquidating." They were used to provide funds for businesses to buy inventory, the value of which was pledged to guarantee repayment of the loans and thereby make them safe loans for bankers to issue. When the inventory was sold by businesses, the funds were generated to repay the loans.

Thus, the standard for a well-managed bank was close adherence to the commercial loan theory. Evidence of this good management was a bank portfolio of assets that consisted of a large portion of commercial loans. The contract or promise to pay held by banks as the financial instrument representing the loans was called *commercial paper*.

However, because commercial loans are not *perfectly* liquid, even a well-managed bank could face the shock of a run on the bank and a shortage of liquidity. Before 1914 and the establishment of the Federal Reserve, the only solution to this situation was for the illiquid bank to borrow from other banks. If the cash drain out of the banks by the public was general and widespread, this was indeed a problem. In the face of such a run on a large segment of the banking system, usually only two solutions were available to avoid insolvency: (1) suspension of payments in cash, and (2) issuance of clearinghouse certificates.

1. Suspension. When bank withdrawals were large and widespread, a general agreement throughout the banking system to suspend payments of cash to customers was often the solution. In the face of a general panic by depositors (a bank run), banks would impose a cooling-off period. Banks would stay open and continue to carry on normal business, except for the fact that no currency would be paid out. Since the banking panic was usually a liquidity crisis based upon rumor of impending failure or a financial scandal involving only a small number of banks, depositors soon came to their senses and the suspension was removed after only one or two days. The fortunate result was that banks had been sheltered from the crisis, and a short-term liquidity problem was not allowed to be transformed into a general inability of banks to pay their customers. Thus, there was no widespread insolvency, no bankruptcy, nor the inevitable result of closing many banks important to their communities.

2. Clearinghouse Banks. These banks were most often the largest and most important banks in a community. Bank representatives met daily at the clearinghouse. They cleared checks for themselves and represented other banks in the process. In the course of business, banks received the checks of other banks from their customers. These checks became assets to the banks that accepted them and a credit to the accounts of their depositors. To efficiently handle the payments by the banks upon which the checks were drawn and for whom they represent liabilities, the clearinghouse was formed. At the meeting of the clearinghouse banks, stocks of checks held by the participants for themselves and as agents for other banks would be exchanged, and at the conclusion of the clearing session, a net payment would be made on the balances existing between the banks.

Clearinghouse banks issued clearinghouse certificates. These certificates were a method for the clearinghouse banks to protect the system from liquidity crises. State and federal banking authorities require that banks hold a minimum supply of reserves and can close banks that do not meet these reserve requirements. The clearinghouse certificates were credit money created by the clearinghouse to serve as bank reserves for banks under pressure of large withdrawals. Of course, the currency and gold coins of the day paid out to depositors lined up at tellers' windows demanding the banks' scarce stock of liquidity also represented reserves assets. Clearinghouse certificates were not only a form of credit designed to restore bank reserves, they were also assets that could be used to obtain currency to meet the demands of customers. In effect they were a means of using credit to expand the money supply temporarily in order to weather the bank runs. Once customers saw they could be paid and trust was restored in the banks, they would put their funds back into the banks. This happened, of course, because checking accounts are more efficient and convenient than currency. We are customers of banks because we need and want checking accounts, at least as long as we have trust in their safety.

With the establishment of the Federal Reserve, loans from the Federal Reserve district banks became the solution provided by Congress to prevent banking liquidity shortages generated by financial crises. The Federal Reserve banks can *create* money and bank reserves! In 1914, their ability to expand bank reserves and the money supply was limited only by the reserves the district banks themselves held. A large portion of these reserves was in the form of gold. A 40 percent backing in gold was required by Congress for each dollar of bank reserves the Federal Reserve created.

The problem for the Federal Reserve was to make sure they were helping the good guys, the banks that were well managed. Federal Reserve banks were authorized to lend to banks facing illiquidity because Congress had realized that such crises created financial instability that could not be tolerated for long. The United States had experienced six major banking crises in the previous 40 years (the most recent in 1907). The 1907 crisis led to the establishment of a presidential commission to search for an answer to the problem. Ultimately, the Federal Reserve Act of 1913 was that answer (government did not move quickly in those days either!). The means to expand credit in the face of a financial crisis, the lending procedure, was called the *discount mechanism*. Banks would borrow from the Federal Reserve banks through the discount window.

We should note as an important aside that the purpose of this expansion of credit was not to expand the economy. Today, we think that one of the main purposes of monetary policy carried out by the Federal Reserve is macroeconomic stabilization. By this, we mean attempting to achieve full employment, a stable price level, and growth of national production. We call this *macroeconomic policy*. However, this was not a goal envisioned in the Federal Reserve Act of 1913. Careful reading of the preamble to the act quoted above would find justification for macroeconomic policy only under "other purposes."

In fact, the word *macroeconomics* had not even been created by 1929, let alone the concept of macroeconomic policy. In those days, economists tended to study "business cycles" and, like the weatherman, tried to understand and even predict the ups and downs of these cycles, but they did not expect to do much about changing them through policy. The point is this: Federal Reserve policy was devised with the goal of stability for banks and the financial system in mind, not the stability of the overall macroeconomy.

The Federal Reserve's mandate was to help save the banks. In addition, the Federal Reserve Act gave the Federal Reserve the power and responsibility for better regulation of banks and the banking industry. These two missions gave rise to an important question and conflict for the Federal Reserve officials: they were to supply credit to banks, but they were also expected to see that banks were properly regulated, which they interpreted in terms of bank management. They believed the Federal Reserve should lend to, and thus encourage, banks that were well managed and faced true liquidity problems. This meant not lending to those banks that were poorly run and were actually insolvent because their assets had lost value relative to their liabilities. The dilemma for the Federal Reserve was to decide which banks were well managed and which ones were not. How could they distinguish the deserving from the undeserving?

The Federal Reserve needed a criterion, a principle of choice, perhaps even a bureaucratic rule for behavior. They chose to use the real bills doctrine. This is perhaps a classic example of both the danger and power of ideas—or at least it exemplifies the danger of acting on an idea not well examined.

At first glance, the underlying logic and economic thought behind the real bills doctrine seem to make a lot of sense. The real bills doctrine had as its basis the undisputed virtue of the commercial loan theory. If the Federal Reserve should help good, well-managed banks, and they are the ones that make short-term commercial loans, then the Fed should lend to them in times of liquidity crisis. Evidence that a bank followed the rules of commercial loan theory was provided by the existence of a large stock of commercial paper in the accounts of the bank. Commercial paper, or real bills, then provided both the rule of behavior for the Federal Reserve and the criterion for separating the good guys from the bad. The collateral approved by the Federal Reserve for loans to banks through the discount window was called *eligible paper*. Eligible paper was usually expected to be short-term securities, such as commercial paper, but this was at the discretion of the Federal Reserve.

It was *always* acceptable for the Federal Reserve to lend to banks that pledged commercial paper as collateral for the loans. This was not only because the eligible paper proved the banks were well managed, but also because the process contributed to another goal of the Federal Reserve: to supply credit needed by businesses to keep production and the economy operating. They called this *meeting the needs of trade*. This was considered a good productive use of credit as opposed to the destructive use of credit for stock market and other forms of speculation.

Unfortunately, the real bills doctrine also had macroeconomic implications that were not so positive. When the economy was expanding, businesses demanded larger and larger amounts of credit because the demand for goods by the public was already growing. When times were bad, businesses reduced their demand for credit and contracted inventory stocks and production. This means that the quantity of commercial paper is procyclical, that is, it moves up and down in conjunction with economic output. Thus, the effect of the Federal Reserve following the real bills doctrine and passively meeting the needs of trade was to expand credit in the face of a growing economy and to cut back supplies of credit in a declining economy.

This is the opposite behavior from that we normally expect from the Federal Reserve today. They are expected to stabilize economic conditions by smoothing out the business cycle with countercyclical policy. This means slowing down the economy when it is growing too fast and, when it is too slow, speeding up economic activity by expanding credit. Therefore, following the real bills doctrine caused the Federal Reserve to follow procyclical monetary policy. In the face of a declining economy during the early 1930s, applying the rules of the real bills doctrine would cause the decline to worsen.

However, this is not the worst of the bad news. The real bills doctrine in its first practical test in an actual liquidity crisis failed in all respects. In

October 1930, a rash of bank runs began in the Midwest. In Arkansas, Missouri, Illinois, Indiana, and Iowa many small banks were faced with large currency drains as the public began to demand repayment of their funds. These banks turned to the Federal Reserve for help and asked for loans through the discount window.

The Federal Reserve refused for two reasons. First, these banks were not members of the Federal Reserve system. They were state-chartered banks, generally located in small rural communities. Their customers were mainly farmers, not businesses. This meant that a very small part of their loan portfolio took the form of short-term commercial loans. Therefore, they had little commercial paper to pledge as collateral to the Federal Reserve's discount window, which provided the second reason to refuse to lend to these banks. Using the criterion of the real bills doctrine, the Federal Reserve concluded that these banks were poorly managed. This fact, along with the position that nonmember banks were not their responsibility, provided the justification for the Federal Reserve to refuse the banks' requests for credit, and many were allowed to fail. Between September and December of 1930, 608 mostly smaller midwestern banks failed, representing $550 million of deposits (Friedman and Schwartz 1963, 308). A total of 1,350 banks were suspended from operation during 1930, of which 1,162 were nonmember banks.[1]

This does not seem to be a world-shaking event. Certainly, it would not appear to be the kind of watershed that we are looking for to explain the transformation of the U.S. recession of 1929 into the nightmare of the Great Depression. However, as we learn early in life, from tiny acorns, mighty oaks grow. During the next three years, lack of confidence in the U.S. banking system led Americans to generate two more major banking crises (1931 and 1932–33). Each successive bank run was worse than the previous one. In 1931, 1932, and 1933 there were 2,293, 1,493, and 4,000 bank failures. By the spring of 1933, almost 11,400 U.S. banks had failed. This was a failure of *45 percent* of the 25,330 banks that had been in business in the spring of 1928 (Federal Reserve Board of Governors, 1943, 283). An insignificant snowball had started down the hill in October 1930, and by 1933 it had been allowed to produce an avalanche of failures.

In March 1931 a more general bank run began across the country. The banks facing this crisis represented a broad range of mainstream conventional commercial banks, many of which were members of the Federal Reserve system. Still, the Federal Reserve refused to lend to them, and many failed. Were they poorly managed? Perhaps some were, but this was a liquidity crisis, and later evidence showed most to have been solvent. Remember, the Federal Reserve's criterion for lending was commercial paper available to be pledged as collateral. The United States had been in a recession for well over a year at this point, and during the recession "the needs of trade" became smaller. Businesses were reducing inventories, not expanding them, so the demand for commercial bank credit was declining, and therefore the stocks of commercial paper were also shrinking in the portfolios of the banks.

In addition, commercial paper represented some of the most liquid assets the banks had available to meet the demands for payment in currency by their depositors. These assets could be quickly sold in the financial markets to raise cash. Thus, the banks that faced runs used the commercial paper they had very quickly and had precious little left to satisfy the Federal Reserve's requirements for collateral. This raises the question of whether the Federal Reserve had any choice in their refusals to lend.

———————

[A]ny Federal reserve bank may discount notes, drafts and bills of exchange arising out of actual commercial transaction; . . . drawn for agricultural, industrial, or commercial purposes, the Federal Reserve Board to have the right to determine or define the character of the paper thus eligible for discount . . . Nothing in this Act shall be construed to prohibit . . . [discounting] bonds and notes of the Government of the United States.

—*Section 13, H.R. 7837,*
Federal Reserve Act 1913, 263–64

———————

Thus, we see the irony of a Federal Reserve system established by Congress less than twenty years before to supply liquidity, to provide an "elastic currency," and to lend to banks in the face of a financial crisis, refusing to lend. The Federal Reserve failed in its first real test. Since they were not lending, did cash-short banks have any other options? They would have under the old clearinghouse system, in which they could have borrowed clearinghouse certificates. But a further irony is the fact that the very existence of the Federal Reserve caused banks to wait for the central bank to act and not turn to the solution they had devised in the face of the banking crises of the nineteenth century. There also was no suspension of payments. The clearinghouse banks looked to the Federal Reserve to act and did not create clearinghouse certificates or lend to the banks under pressure of withdrawals. They stood by and waited forlornly for the rescue that never came.

With the failure of 11,000 banks, the depositors' accounts were lost and money and savings destroyed. Many of the banks were ultimately able to pay their depositors almost all of their funds, but this happened years later. In the meantime, the U.S. money supply fell precipitously. In three years, the U.S. stock of money fell 33 percent in nominal terms, which helped cause national income to fall by 53 percent (Friedman and Schwartz 1963, 301–2). As we have seen, the direct result was falling consumer expenditures and business investment, which led to the loss of millions of jobs.

The real bills doctrine, that seemingly innocuous Federal Reserve decision rule designed to achieve reasonable and defensible goals, and the officials who applied it must take the blame for perhaps the greatest economic disaster in history. This is truly an example of both the power and the danger of ideas!

6.2. The Worldwide Depression

To answer the second question, about why the Great Depression was a worldwide event, we must return to the gold standard. With the downturn in the U.S. economy in 1929, a lower level of national income led to less demand for goods by U.S. consumers and businesses. Obviously, a fall in demand for foreign goods was included in this decline. Thus, the value of U.S. imports fell from $5.5 billion in 1928 to $1.9 billion by 1932 (Balke and Gordon 1986). The result was an increasing surplus in the U.S. balance of payments, then, in turn, increasingly large inflows of gold-denominated payments from our net surplus of U.S. exports over imports.

It might seem like this should be good for helping to reverse the U.S. depression, but as we will see, it did not have this effect. More to the point, the U.S. gold inflow meant large outflows of gold from Europe. The supply of gold in Europe declined, and so did their money supplies. With less money, less consumer and business demand for goods and services was generated, and Europe found itself falling into its own depression.

Falling prices would be expected to correct that problem automatically, perhaps before too long had passed. But the industrial economies of North America and Europe in 1929–30 generated two severe additional problems. Rising unemployment occurred along with falling prices, and the period of adjustment out of the depression and back to full employment lengthened unbearably.

In the mainly agrarian world of the nineteenth century, prices in freely competitive commodity markets would have fallen more easily than the prices of manufactured goods did in the industrial world of the twentieth century. Firms did not just auction off their industrial goods in a commodity market, as farmers would have done with their corn.

Fixed costs of capital and difficulties in cutting wages in hard times tended to cause firms to cut production rather than reduce prices to levels low enough to clear the market. Thus, when a trade deficit produced gold outflows and then, in turn, falling money stocks, the general result began to be declining national incomes and rising unemployment. What could European governments do to counteract a loss of gold like the one they faced in 1929–30?

As long as each country stayed on the gold standard and followed its rules, there was nothing they could do. Less gold meant less money, and the rules of the game did not allow governments to print paper money that was not backed by gold. Governments had to accept the consequences of the outflow of gold or quit the gold standard. Because Great Britain had faced a similar situation during the 1920s brought on by their own misguided policies designed to restore the gold standard after World War I, they were not prone to repeat the experience. Thus, Great Britain left the gold standard on September 21, 1931, the first major power to do so.[2]

This allowed the Bank of England to expand the British money supply and thus escape the worst effects of the Great Depression. Because Japan also left gold early in December 1931, these two countries experienced the mildest depressions faced by any of the major industrial countries in the 1930s.

For Germany the experience was different. Because of the hyperinflation and the collapse of the reichsmark in 1923 when they printed reams of paper currency, the German government stayed on the gold standard for several more years. Ironically, the German traumatic experience of the 1920s and their fear of losing the price stability they believed would be ensured by the gold standard caused them to cling to gold. The result was the worst 1930s experience endured in Europe and a Great Depression disaster only exceeded by the situation in the United States. Industrial production fell in Germany by over 50 percent from 1929 to 1933. In contrast it declined between 10 and 20 percent in Great Britain and less than 10 percent in Japan. The United States faced a drop of over 60 percent (Romer 1993, 22).

The description given above of the spread of the Depression from the United States to Europe and our other trading partners would seem a bad enough indictment of the gold standard and its much vaunted reputation for promoting monetary and macroeconomic stability. However, things actually became worse. What we have described is the system as it worked when the rules of the game were followed. The European situation was certainly unenviable given the choice they had: stay with the gold standard, lose gold, and watch prices, output, and employment plunge, with little hope of avoiding high levels of pain and suffering; or go off the gold standard, break the rules of the game, and move into a world of uncertainty and perhaps monetary collapse. Although the latter choice turned out to be the better one, it was a jump into the unknown when each country finally reached that decision. Remember, the gold system was expected ultimately to adjust the balance of payments such that the outflow of gold would stop as U.S. gold stocks rose and began to raise U.S. prices. Because this could be expected to reduce our exports and increase imports, it was merely a question of time until gold flows reversed direction. The question was whether the short-run economic pain and political danger to European governments could be weathered long enough to allow this adjustment. That was the uncertainty.

The answer was ultimately no, but this result turned out to be a direct result of a factor unforeseen in our explanation of the workings of the gold standard. The United States did not follow the rules of the game. This would seem to be rather strange. After all, the United States was under no pressure of lost gold. The adjustment should have been aiding the stabilization of our economy. Falling prices should have begun to rise as our trade surplus generated large gold inflows. These inflows were $175.1 million in 1929 and $280.1 million in 1930. The movement of gold alone should have raised the monetary base, bank reserves, and the money supply as much as 19 percent. Not only would this have helped reverse the fall in prices, demand for goods, and thus employment, it should also have helped our banks weather the liquidity crises. It should have helped save many from failure in the face of the bank runs and little help from a Federal Reserve enamored of the real bills doctrine. It should have done all of this, but it did not. Instead, the U.S. money supply *fell* by 3.75 percent from December 31, 1928, to December 31, 1930.

To understand why none of the predicted results came about, it is necessary to take a step back in time to the first years of the Federal Reserve. In 1914, the Europeans had begun the four-year struggle of World War I, but the United States was still a neutral party. The benefits of wartime trade were already generating tremendous increases in U.S. exports of grain and arms to Europe. The average U.S. annual net export position rose almost 5,000 percent from the 1911–14 period to the 1914–18 period. This represented an increase in the average U.S. trade surplus from $61 million per year to $3.033 billion per year (in real 1929 dollars), which produced a huge gold flow into the United States (U.S. Department of Commerce 1966, 171). From 1914 to 1918 the U.S. gold stock increased from $1.526 billion to $2.873 billion.

The Federal Reserve recognized that the effect of this would be severe inflation in the short run, which would in the long run price our goods out of the postwar markets and cause the gold to return to Europe. The U.S. Treasury asked itself why we should have to go through all of this just because the Europeans were fighting a war of which we had no part.

Therefore, the Federal Reserve undertook to prevent the inflation from occurring. They did this by breaking the rules of the game and sterilizing the gold flows so that they could not infect our economy with inflationary money. This was done by having the Federal Reserve sell U.S. Treasury bonds in the open market. Sales of the bonds generated payments to the Federal Reserve District Banks in the form of bank demand deposits.

These checks, when cashed by the Federal Reserve, led to payment by banks to the Federal Reserve. The purchasers of the bonds would have their accounts debited and the proceeds would be transferred to the Federal Reserve's account. This would cause a transfer of bank reserves to the Federal Reserve in the form of gold deposits, and the net result would be a decline in the ability of banks to create demand deposits and thus a decline in the money supply. Unfortunately, Federal Reserve officials had discovered that they could sterilize the gold that flowed into the United States by removing it from the banking system, thereby preventing the expansion of the U.S. money supply. With no more money in the system, there was no increase in public demand for goods and services and no undesirable increase in the price level. Inflation was prevented. It worked.

Given this experience with sterilization, the Federal Reserve was well prepared to repeat the experiment in 1929 through 1933. The obvious question is: why would they want to sterilize gold inflows in the midst of a Depression, and with accelerating bank liquidity crises? One would think the resulting increase in the U.S. money supply and bank reserves would be viewed as manna from heaven. What could be better than a larger money stock leading to a reversal of falling prices and employment, which also supplied the gold reserves needed by banks to face the huge withdrawals produced by the bank runs?

Unfortunately, the Federal Reserve did not see it this way. As far as they were concerned, banks were failing because they were poorly managed. In addition, the real bills doctrine directed that credit could be increased only to meet the needs of trade. In a declining economy, credit and money expansion was not seen by the Federal Reserve as meeting the needs of trade. It was thought to promote instead the kind of stock market speculation and "inflation" faced in the 1920s. Many in the Federal Reserve system and elsewhere confused the speculative rise in the stock market with inflation, which is in fact a rise in the general level of prices of goods and services in the economy. This is obviously not the same thing at all (Friedman and Schwartz 1963, 407–8).

So every ounce of gold that flowed in from Europe and elsewhere was sterilized. The result of this was obviously bad for the U.S. economy, but it was even worse for our European trading partners. There was no automatic mechanism to bring a halt to the outflow of gold and money from Europe and thereby end their Depression. Prices were not allowed to rise in the United States. European exports did not rise. The gold did not flow back to Europe, and the shortage of credit and money was not corrected.

As long as European countries remained on the gold standard and U.S. sterilization continued, there could be no end of the Depression in sight. The U.S. gold stock would become a huge pile of sterilized and useless gold. Starting with the British in 1931, our trading partners began to recognize this fact, and one by one they left the gold standard. The Germans and, ironically, the United States were among the last to leave gold and so were hurt the worst, experiencing the longest and deepest forms of the Depression.

CHAPTER 7

1931: The Make-or-Break Year

—————— ➤•◦•◄ ——————

At its January 1931 meeting, the [Federal Reserve's] Open Market Policy Conference recommended that "it would be desirable to dispose of some of the System holdings of government securities" . . . the Board approved the conference's recommendation and, by February 1931, security holdings had fallen by $130 million.

—Milton Friedman and Anna J. Schwartz, relating the Federal Reserve's strange decision to further tighten credit conditions in early 1931 (1963, 377)

Imagine how a loss of 15 to 20 percent of deposits within a two year period [from 1929–31], with prospects of more losses to come, would drain a bank's reserves and other liquid assets, put it under more pressure to contract loans, and reduce its ability to withstand runs.

—Lester Chandler (1970, 81)

—————— ➤•◦•◄ ——————

By the beginning of 1931 the industrialized countries of the world were in the midst of very serious economic recessions. In varying degrees countries were experiencing falling output and prices in addition to massive unemployment. The year 1931 turned out to be an especially important one during the Great Depression. This was the year when a bank run in Austria set off a worldwide financial crisis that initiated a sequence of events that accelerated the economic decline in many countries. This financial crisis, which set off a series of runs on foreign capital in several countries, placed the governments of industrialized countries in a position where they were faced with a decision: either (1) pursue contractionary monetary policies in an effort to protect their currency's value and stem the gold outflow, or (2) abandon the gold standard and allow their currency to float in value. Countries that chose the former option of raising interest rates (for example, the United States and Germany) pursued contractionary monetary policies that caused their economies to slip further into even deeper, longer Depressions. Those that chose to abandon the gold standard (for example, Britain and Japan) were able to follow expansionary monetary policies and climb out of their depressions much sooner.

7.1. The Slide Continues

A long line of customers were waiting to withdraw their bank deposits when the armored truck pulled up. The desperate bank manager ran out to the truck. "Are you from the Federal Reserve?" he asked the driver. The driver replied that yes, he had been sent by the Federal Reserve. "Thank God!" cried the bank manager. "We have a run going on. Bring the cash in quickly through the back door, we are in great need." The driver looked at the manager for a moment. "We're not here to give you cash, we're here to take it. You have deficient reserves this month!"
—*A story that made the rounds during the 1930s*

There were apparently two major reasons why the world economies continued to slide during 1931. First was the monetary policy being carried out in the United States and other countries. In the United States, the money stock fell nearly 7.0 percent during the year, but the rate varied considerably over the course of the year. The money stock actually rose slightly during the first few months because confidence in the banking system returned as the effects of the 1930 bank failures abated. The public was willing to hold more bank deposits relative to currency and so the money multiplier rose, enough to offset the Federal Reserve's sterilization of the gold inflow that was occurring at the time. This sterilization took the form of sales of securities by the Federal Reserve.

Why was the Federal Reserve selling bonds in the midst of a serious recession? The answer is that most officials in the organization thought that inflationary credit conditions existed, when in fact credit conditions were very tight. The manner in which they reached this incorrect conclusion is made clear by letters between Federal Reserve officials during a discussion about the proper course of monetary policy during the summer of 1930. The proof to Federal Reserve officials that credit conditions were easy was the fact that money market interest rates were low. Friedman and Schwartz cite the views of several of the Federal Reserve Banks' presidents on this issue (1963, 370–73). For example, George Norris, president of the Philadelphia Federal Reserve Bank, was convinced of the "unwisdom of attempting to depress still further the abnormally low interest rates now prevailing." John Caulkins, president of the San Francisco Federal Reserve Bank, claimed that "with credit cheap and redundant we do not believe that business recovery will be accelerated by making credit cheaper and more redundant." W. B. Geery of the Minneapolis Federal Reserve was concerned about the "danger of stimulating financing which will lead to still more overproduction while attempting to make it easy to do financing which will increase consumption."

It is true that money market interest rates had fallen substantially since 1929. For example, commercial paper rates had been in the 6.0 percent range during 1929 and by early 1931 had fallen below 3.0 percent. By the summer of 1931 they were at 2.0 percent. Yet it is important to realize that there were other reasons for the rate decline besides the Federal Reserve's explanation that it resulted from easy credit conditions. In fact, the true situation is shown in figure 7.1, which shows the supply and demand for money. When the monetary contraction began in 1928, money market interest rates rose. Then, when the recession started, income and prices fell. Since the demand for nominal money balances depends on nominal income, falling output and prices reduced the demand for money. Thus, the demand schedule shifted to the left further than the supply schedule, and short-term interest rates fell. In this way, the low money market interest rates were indicative of extremely tight credit conditions, not easy as the Federal Reserve maintained.

In the midst of the Federal Reserve's "easy credit" policy another wave of bank panics began. This wave started in March 1931 and proved to be much more serious than the failures during the previous year. The precipitating factors that started this wave are not clear, but Chandler makes a persuasive case that it was caused by a combination of deteriorating asset quality in the form of bad loans at banks located in the geographic areas that were hit hardest by the recession (agricultural areas and the industrial upper Midwest) and a net outflow of funds from those areas to certain more prosperous urban areas (such as New York) (1970,

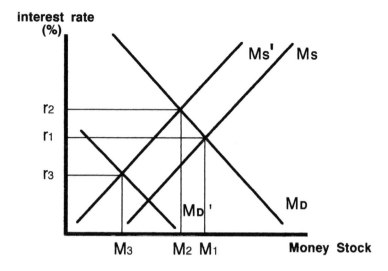

Fig. 7.1.   Short-term interest rates were low because the demand for money fell

77–84). This shift in funds occurred because those areas hit hardest by the Depression were suffering the largest income declines. As their incomes fell, so did their bank deposits, which greatly weakened the banks in those regions. Chandler argues that as those banks' credit positions deteriorated, the money center banks in New York and Chicago were increasingly reluctant to extend credit to the weakening smaller banks.

This wave of failures was much more serious than the 1930 wave because it lasted longer, starting in March and persisting throughout the year. In addition, many more banks failed than in 1930. To cite a few examples, during 1931 the failure rates were 15.2 percent of all banks operating in Michigan, 16.6 percent in Iowa, 18.2 percent in Mississippi, and 18.9 percent in South Dakota (Chandler 1970, 83–84). In addition, the public reaction to this wave of failures was much stronger than it had been during the previous year. The money multiplier, which was virtually unchanged during 1930, fell 23 percent during 1931 as the public converted bank deposits into currency. As a result, the U.S. money stock fell 5.25 percent from March to August and then another 12.0 percent from August to January 1932.

The second reason the economy continued to plummet during 1931 was the continuing deflation brought on by the falling stock of money.

The GDP deflator, an index of the overall price level, had fallen 3.3 percent during 1930. It fell 8.8 percent during 1931. The deflation continued in other countries as well; during 1931 wholesale prices fell 12 percent in Germany, 9.8 percent in France, and 17.9 percent in Britain.[1] As a result, debt became increasingly burdensome to debtors virtually throughout the world.

7.2. The World Financial Crisis

The worsening economic situation during the latter months of 1931 was associated with the worldwide financial crisis that came to a head during September of that year. This financial crisis started in May with the collapse of the KreditAnstalt, Austria's largest bank. Austria's economy had been in poor shape since World War I, and as a result, many small banks in weak financial positions had merged with larger banks. The KreditAnstalt was one of these larger banks, and as it absorbed other banks it became quite large—by 1929 it owned 60 percent of the equity of Austrian industries (Kindleberger 1986, 145). Unfortunately, one of the larger banks it merged with turned out to have falsely reported its loan losses. When auditors finally discovered the true situation, they reported that the KreditAnstalt was accumulating large losses. A consortium consisting of the Austrian government, the Austrian National Bank, and the House of Rothschild started a rescue operation for the KreditAnstalt. However, when news got out that the bank needed help, a run began on the bank. With the collapse of Austria's largest bank, a capital flight from Austria occurred.

The bank runs spread to Germany, and banks there were forced to close down by the middle of June. The situation had been made worse by an announcement by Chancellor Bruning on June 5 that Germany was no longer going to pay reparations under the Young Plan. He said a new schedule of payments was necessary. As a result, foreigners began to pull their capital out of Germany. Germany was in an especially vulnerable position because of changes in the banking system that had taken place there during the 1920s. German banks had become increasingly dependent upon short-term foreign credits, had acquired increasingly illiquid assets, and had reduced their holdings of capital (Hardach 1984, 214–15). As a result, foreigners were able to pull out their short-term holdings very quickly, and when they did the German banks were severely weakened. Several German banks collapsed as a result. The crisis was worsened by the fact that the central bank could not accept government securities as collateral for discounts. After the hyperinflation during the 1920s the German government had passed a law prohibiting the monetization of government debt.

The response of Germany's central bank to the crisis was an attempt to stop the capital and gold outflow by raising interest rates. The discount rate, which was just under 5.0 percent at the start of the year, stood at 10 percent during the height of the crisis in July. By the end of the year, it had fallen to 8.0 percent. In addition, the public responded to the bank failures by reducing their holdings of bank deposits. Commercial bank deposits in 1931 were 33 percent below the 1930 level. The German economy plummeted.

The crisis continued to spread. In late June, Germany had temporarily frozen foreign credits, that is, payments from German firms for goods received from businesses in other countries. As a result, many of the smaller European countries' banks were temporarily short of liquid assets and had to look elsewhere for funds. Many of these banks had accounts in London banks, and they began to sell their British pound assets for gold (Kindleberger 1986, 154). By early July this wave of selling was placing pressure upon the pound, and foreign investors were beginning to lose confidence in that currency. Then, the pressure on the pound intensified on July 23 when the Macmillan Report (originally commissioned in 1929) on Britain's international finances was released. The report pointed out that Britain's short-term liabilities to foreigners were several times the country's gold reserves. In other words, Britain did not have enough gold reserves if foreigners tried to convert all of their pound-denominated assets into gold.

The situation deteriorated further in August and September as Britain careened through a series of political crises. The ruling Labour party fell from power on August 24 over the issue of spending cuts. The problem was that Britain wanted to borrow from abroad to help defend the pound, but as a condition for the loan the British government had to reduce its budget deficit. The Labour party Chancellor of the Exchequer, Philip Snowden, proposed a 10 percent cut in unemployment compensation benefits as well as salary cuts for government employees, including those in the military. This proposal to cut unemployment compensation benefits flew in the face of the prevailing philosophy of the Labour party and this led to the party resigning from power (Rolfe and Burtle 1973, 30–31). The Labour party was replaced by a coalition government that made further efforts to cut salaries of government employees. The icing on the cake occurred on September 15 when sailors in the Royal Navy held a protest over the proposed pay cuts. This protest was written up in the London newspapers as a mutiny in the Navy! As Kindleberger points out, "if the Royal Navy were to go, how long would that other mainstay of nineteenth-century liberalism last—the gold standard run by the City of London?" (1986, 156). The selling of pounds continued at an even faster pace; it had become a full-blown currency run.[2]

Britain tried to defend the pound, but the Bank of England's options were limited.[3] The basic problem was that stopping the outflow required a major hike in interest rates. But that would be a contractionary policy, and with the unemployment rate already at 20 percent, officials at the Bank of England were not willing to drive the unemployment rate up even higher (Eichengreen 1992b, 282). This left just one other option available if Britain were to remain on the gold standard: borrowing from abroad. Britain turned to the United States and France for help and received a loan worth 50 million pounds in July, but that was used up in three weeks. Total borrowing by Britain from the time the Macmillan Report was issued in July until the gold standard was abandoned in September was about 82 million pounds. This was nowhere near the amount necessary because during that same period the capital outflow was about 200 million pounds (Rolfe and Burtle 1973, 30). Britain tried to borrow more, but as the financial crisis spread to the United States, the Federal Reserve was increasingly reluctant to lend, and the Bank of France insisted that any lending from them be matched by an equal amount from the Federal Reserve (Eichengreen 1992b, 283).

7.3. Britain's Decision

There are few Englishmen who do not rejoice at the breaking of our gold fetters. We feel that we have at last a free hand to do what is sensible. The romantic phase is over, and we can begin to discuss realistically what policy is for the best.
>—*John Maynard Keynes, celebrating Britain's abandonment of the gold standard (1931, 288)*

The first major country to surpass its 1929 performance in industrial production was the United Kingdom, which reached 116 in the last quarter of 1934, compared with 114 in the last quarter of 1929.
>—*Charles P. Kindleberger (1986, 240)*

Figuratively speaking, Britain's back was to the wall. They were unable to obtain further borrowings from foreign central banks and unwilling to pursue contractionary policies to protect their gold stock. There was just one option available: abandon the gold standard. This was done on September 21, 1931, when Britain suspended the conversion of pounds into gold and allowed the pound to float on foreign currency markets. The pound promptly depreciated in value: 25 percent within just a few days and 30 percent by December (Kindleberger 1986, 158–59).[4] An important aspect of Britain's decision to abandon gold was that their quantity of money was no longer tied to their gold stock. In other words, the Bank of England could now pursue expansionary monetary policies and help get Britain out of their recession.

Unfortunately, Britain continued to pursue deflationary monetary policies for a few more months. The Bank of England apparently was concerned that a monetary expansion would set off inflation, but, as Temin notes, they "fought an inflation that did not exist" (1989, 75). The bank believed that tight monetary policies would stabilize the pound at a relatively high value that would result in a favorable exchange rate when they paid back the U.S. and French credits that had been extended during the pound crisis. At the same time, the Treasury favored expansionary monetary policies because they wanted to promote economic recovery while at the same time driving the price level up so as to reduce the real value of their government debt (Kirby 1981, 68). The Treasury eventually won the debate and in February 1932 the Bank of England lowered the bank rate.[5] Then, in April, the Exchange Equalisation Account was set up whereby the Treasury bought and sold Treasury bills to offset capital inflows and outflows in an effort to stabilize the value of the pound. This action was accompanied by another reduction in the bank rate, and then the rate was lowered again in June to 2 percent. It remained at that level until 1939. These actions resulted in an increase in the monetary base during the summer, and the British economic recovery began in August (Richardson 1967, 21).

The recovery resulted in more vibrant growth than had taken place during the 1920s. From 1932 to 1937 industrial production rose 46 percent while real income rose 22 percent. Over that same period employment rose 17 percent although the labor force unemployment rate came down slowly. The unemployment rate, which had been 22.1 percent in 1932, fell to 10.8 percent in 1937 (Richardson 1967, 22). Apparently, a major reason for the unemployment rate staying high was the continuation of the regional pockets of unemployment that had developed during the 1920s in the shipbuilding, textile, and coal industries (Kindleberger 1986, 240).

The recovery was concentrated in the export industries and housing. The depreciation of the pound reduced prices of British goods sold abroad, and exports of chemicals, autos, and electrical equipment enjoyed solid gains (Kindleberger 1986, 242). New home building rose significantly due to a variety of factors including the monetary expansion and associated low interest rates, the apparent peak in a long-term cycle of building, and the increased use of the automobile resulting in the construction of houses on the outskirts of cities (Richardson 1967, 161–67). The housing boom was so strong that it accounted for 20 percent of the total gain in employment from 1932 to 1935 (Richardson 1967, 177). In addition, the rise in home building resulted in gains in production in complementary industries such as home furnishings, bricks, lumber, and plumbing fixtures.

7.4. Runs on the Yen and Dollar

The downside of Britain's move to leave the gold standard was that it raised suspicions that other countries might soon follow the same course and depreciate their currencies as well. When a currency depreciates, the value of foreigners' assets denominated in that currency falls. This was the apparent impetus for runs on other currencies, in particular upon the Japanese yen and the U.S. dollar, which began shortly after Britain left the gold standard. The Japanese also chose to leave the gold standard and pursue highly expansionary policies that Patrick describes as "one of the most successful combinations of fiscal, monetary, and foreign exchange rate policies, in an adverse international environment, the world has ever seen" (1971, 256). Government spending rose 26 percent between 1931 and 1933 with much of that going toward military expenditures (Patrick 1971, 257). The exchange rate depreciated significantly, 50 percent during 1932, and then another 50 percent during 1933 (Nanto and Takagi 1985, 371). Exports growth became very strong as a result. In addition, the central bank gradually reduced the discount rate, but the money supply growth was moderate. Patrick (1971) and Nanto and Takagi (1985) conclude that the Japanese recovery was largely the result of the yen depreciation and expansionary fiscal policy. The economy attained full employment by 1936.

Unlike in the recovering British and Japanese economies, in the United States economic output continued to plummet. Foreigners very quickly had began pulling their financial capital out of the United States just before Britain abandoned the gold standard. Friedman and Schwartz report that the U.S. gold stock declined by $275 million from September 16 to September 30, and then by an additional $450 million during the month of October (1963, 316). Thus, in the span of just one and a half months, the United States lost the entire gold inflow that had taken place during the previous two years.

The Federal Reserve's response to the gold outflow was to attempt to stop it by raising U.S. interest rates. The New York Federal Reserve Bank's discount rate was raised from 1.5 percent to 2.5 percent on October 16, and then to 3.5 percent a week later, "the sharpest rise within so brief a period in the whole history of the System, before or since" (Friedman and Schwartz 1963, 317). There was apparently never any discussion of the United States dropping the gold standard. In fact, the move to defend gold was widely applauded around the country (Friedman and Schwartz 1963, 382).

7.5.   Bagehot's Advice

Very large loans at very high rates are the best remedy for the worst malady of the money market when a foreign drain is added to a domestic drain. Any notion that money is not to be had, or that it may not be had at any price, only raises alarm to panic and enhances panic to madness.

> —*Walter Bagehot describing what became*
> *known as his Golden Rule for dealing with a*
> *combined gold outflow and domestic bank*
> *deposit withdrawal (1873, 75)*

Walter Bagehot was famous in nineteenth-century British politics and finance. For many years he served as editor of *The Economist*, which was then, and still is, one of the world's preeminent publications in politics and economics. In 1873, his book *Lombard Street* was published. The book is named after the street where the Bank of England is located, in the center of London's financial district. This book went on to become known as the bible for central bankers. In it Bagehot explains what a central bank should do when a country is simultaneously experiencing a gold outflow and large withdrawals of bank deposits or bank runs: lend freely at high interest rates. The idea is to raise interest rates to stop the gold outflow, but at the same time keep the bank withdrawals from causing banks to collapse by lending bank reserves (discounts) to any bank that asks. In addition, the central bank should not be too choosy about what they accept as collateral for the discounts.

Bagehot's advice was badly needed in the autumn of 1931, for the United States was experiencing the exact situation he described. Banks had been experiencing deposit withdrawals since March, and the situation was just getting worse as the public heard of more and more banks failing. Then, in mid-September the gold outflow began. What the Federal Reserve needed to do was raise the discount rate to help stop the gold outflow and at the same time discount freely to banks and expand the list of acceptable collateral for those discounts to include a wide variety of financial assets. That way the gold outflow could be stopped and further bank failures prevented.

Unfortunately, the Federal Reserve followed only half of Bagehot's advice. They raised the discount rate to stop the gold outflow, but did not discount freely the way Bagehot advised. The Federal Reserve made discounts available, but only to banks that offered the right kind of collateral: commercial paper. This was the real bills doctrine in action; eligible paper was commercial paper. The problem was that there simply was not much commercial paper outstanding by 1931. Commercial paper is short-term debt, typically used to finance business inventory holdings. As the general decline in business had continued since 1929, firms had been selling off their inventories; as they did so the need for commercial paper diminished. So the collateral required of the banking system in order to obtain discounts from the Federal Reserve was in short supply. As the year wore on, the public saw more and more banks fail, and they became increasingly concerned about the safety of their deposits. Many banks desperately needed reserves but did not have the collateral the Federal Reserve considered acceptable. In addition, many of the banks failing were not members of the Federal Reserve system. Federal Reserve officials did not consider themselves responsible for nonmember banks.

Because of these factors, the bank failures increased, the public continued to convert deposits into currency, and the stock of money plummeted. From August 1931 until the banking crisis abated in January 1932, the money multiplier fell 16.4 percent, and almost all of this decline was caused by the conversion of bank deposits into currency. So while the monetary base rose 4.4 percent during that period, the money stock fell 12 percent, "or at the annual rate of 31 percent—a rate of decline larger by far for any comparable span in the 53 years for which we have monthly data, and in the whole 93-year period for which we have a continuous series on the money stock" (Friedman and Schwartz 1963, 318).

As a result of the major decline in the stock of money and associated decline in consumer and business confidence, U.S. economic activity plunged, especially in the cyclically sensitive industries. The Federal Reserve's Index of Industrial Production fell 29 percent during the course of the year, while real GNP fell 8 percent and the price deflator dropped 8.8 percent. The unemployment rate, which averaged 8.9 percent during 1930, was 16.3 percent during 1931.[6]

Meanwhile, many other industrialized countries' economies were experiencing sharp downturns as well. German industrial production, which had risen slightly during the first six months of 1931, plummeted 24 percent during the last half of the year. During 1931 industrial production in France fell 18 percent over the course of the year, in Chile it dropped 26 percent, in Austria it fell 13 percent, and in Canada it declined 30 percent during just the last seven months of the year.[7] The Soviet Union was the only country tracked by the League of Nations that experienced rising output in 1931.[8]

Thus, 1931 was important because it was the year when the major recessions in the industrialized countries significantly deepened. The causes of this debacle were fragile banking systems in many countries combined with perverse monetary policies that were focused on trying to maintain the gold standard. Countries that abandoned the gold standard unshackled themselves from the system and were able to pursue policies that allowed their economies to expand and the misery to end. But many other countries stayed with the system and were doomed to many more months of falling output and rising poverty.

CHAPTER 8

More Bank Failures, 1932–33

Were we trying to wreck the financial structure of the nation in trying to protect ourselves against this disaster? I suppose we were. But the small sum of money we had in those banks was all that stood between us and the bread line. We figured that it might last us a year if we counted the pennies and did not get sick. My husband had been unable to find employment. Our investments had become worthless. We could not have sold the house at any price, or rented it for enough to keep us, and we could not possibly have mortgaged it. If we had lost what little ready cash we had, there was no one who would or could have paid our grocery bills or bought us coal against the blizzards. By Thursday of that week we had done everything we could with our own affairs. Friday there was nothing to do but watch—watch the bottom drop out of the world we knew. We saw the runs on the big Loop banks. We saw the city [of Chicago], at first hysterical, then stunned—prostrate. I shall never see an armored truck again without a shudder at the memory of that day.

> —*Louise Armstrong explaining why she and her husband withdrew their bank deposits on Thursday, February 16, 1933, and what happened the following day (1938, 49–50)*

At the end of 1931 the U.S. economy was in dire straights. Millions of people were unemployed, a great many firms and farmers were either bankrupt or close to it, and the banks that had been fortunate enough to survive during 1931 were in very weak positions. In short, the U.S. economy was on the brink of disaster, and in several other countries the situation was no better. Yet conditions became even worse. Due to a combination of economic ignorance, confusion, and incompetence, U.S. policymakers pursued policies that were highly contractionary. They deepened and transformed the recession into a Great Depression.

8.1. Herbert Hoover

As I look back over our whole era of boom and slump, and our passage through the valley of the shadow after the European panic [of 1931], I feel that our own banking and financial system was the worst part of the dismal tragedy with which I had to deal.

—Herbert Hoover (1952, 21)

Herbert Hoover (1874–1964) is a somewhat maligned character in American history. He was a very accomplished man who had a world-wide reputation as a mining engineer. In addition, he had led food relief efforts in China after the Boxer Rebellion and in Europe after World War I. Those efforts saved countless thousands of lives. He was also present at the peace negotiations following World War I. There, Hoover earned the respect and admiration of John Maynard Keynes for advocating compassion toward Germany.

Unfortunately for Hoover, however, his life's work of good deeds is largely forgotten because he was president of the United States from 1929 to 1933, and as such had the misfortune to be in office during the big slide. Many Americans at the time considered Hoover a weak, incompetent man, who was responsible for the Depression. In fact, there were many camps around the country where unemployed, destitute people were forced to live in tents. These camps were called "Hoovervilles." While Hoover was partly responsible for the problem, in fairness the Federal Reserve clearly deserved much more of the blame. By all rights those tent camps should have been called "Federalreservevilles."

In terms of his economic thinking, Hoover was very much a man of his times. He accepted the prevailing wisdom of the day: economic recessions were just a part of the natural order of things and must be endured periodically. The idea was that the economy naturally cycled up and down and that the down periods were mild and short-lived. So when the economy began to slide in 1929, Hoover's reaction was to do nothing: to leave it alone, believing it would self-correct in short order. When the downturn continued during 1930, Hoover's reaction was still to take no major action. However, when the bank failures intensified during the autumn of 1931, Hoover drew the line. He clearly understood that the bank failures were intensifying the recession, and he considered Federal Reserve inaction to be part of the problem. At that time he also began to advocate establishing federal deposit insurance as a way to stop the bank panics.

Since the Federal Reserve, as lender of last resort, was not going to help the banks, Hoover proposed setting up a government agency to do so. In early 1932 his proposed agency, the Reconstruction Finance Corporation (RFC), received congressional approval. The agency was given $500 million and authorized to borrow an additional $1.5 billion in the form of bonds backed by the U.S. government. The agency was to lend these funds to financial institutions and railroads. In effect, the RFC was to do what the Federal Reserve should have been doing in the first place—extend credit to banks.

However, the RFC turned out to be ineffective because the terms specified for the loans were so strict. Weak banks that needed help the most did not qualify. Furthermore, as banks weakened and sold off bonds to raise cash, bond prices fell. This worsened the situation by further reducing bank assets. The RFC did nothing to keep bond prices from falling. To make matters even worse, an act passed in July 1932 specified that the names of banks borrowing from the RFC must be made public. This discouraged banks from borrowing because they were afraid that the public would (correctly) interpret such information as a sign that the bank was in a weak position and immediately panic and withdraw their funds (Friedman and Schwartz 1963, 325). Hoover's RFC was the right idea, but operationally inadequate.

Hoover is better remembered for his ill-timed tax hike in 1932. As the country plunged into recession the federal budget moved into deficit. Here are the National Income and Product Account current-dollar federal budget net revenue positions from 1929 to 1931:

1929	$1,175 million
1930	$283 million
1931	–$2,134 million

The fiscal position moved from the large surplus in 1929 to the sizable deficit in 1931. This was mainly because tax revenues plummeted from a combination of falling income and lower tax rates legislated in December 1929 (Campagna 1987, 97). Meanwhile, on the spending side, transfer payments rose significantly. In response to demonstrations (some violent), bonus checks, originally scheduled to be paid several years later, were sent out to World War I veterans.

There was a great deal of concern at the time about the large deficit in 1931, enough so that it became a campaign issue in the 1932 election contest between Hoover and Franklin Roosevelt. At the time, it was strict dogma that a government running a deficit was living beyond its means and running counter to the welfare of the country. In Hoover's own words, "national stability required that we balance the budget" (1952, 132). The Hoover administration attempted to balance the budget by raising taxes and cutting spending. Spending in 1932 was about $1 billion lower than in 1931 largely because veterans did not receive bonus checks in 1932. The Revenue Act of 1932 raised tax rates significantly on both personal and corporate income, as well as estates.[1] It became law on June 6, 1932, and was "the largest tax increase in peacetime in the nation's history to that date" (Campagna 1987, 99). In hindsight, the contractionary Revenue Act of 1932 was the wrong medicine at the wrong time. Furthermore, the act did not generate a balanced budget. As the economy continued to plummet, tax revenue fell as well. Yet, given the state of economic knowledge at the time, raising taxes and cutting spending seemed to many people the right thing to do.[2]

8.2. The Open Market Purchase Program

The rate of bank failures slowed at the start of 1932, and the ratio of currency to deposits actually fell slightly during the first three months of the year. In April, however, it began to rise again. As a result, the money multiplier continued to fall during the course of the year. Meanwhile, a continued gold outflow was dragging down the monetary base. Both the falling base and money multiplier caused the stock of money to keep on falling, taking aggregate demand and output down with it.

By the spring of 1932 several members of Congress had become highly irritated with the Federal Reserve, which they partly blamed for the continuing economic decline. Federal Reserve officials, concerned about the possibility of "radical financial legislation by Congress" (Harrison, from Friedman and Schwartz 1963, 384), responded by initiating an open market purchase program in April. The program specified that the Federal Reserve Banks would purchase a total of $500 million worth of securities over the course of five weeks. This action was taken, and in May the Federal Reserve decided to purchase another $500 million worth. This was largely accomplished by the end of June and completed by early August. Thus, in the space of just a few months the Federal Reserve holdings of securities had roughly doubled. They were finally undertaking the kinds of policies needed to halt the economic decline, but only under the threat of congressional action.

The $1 billion increase in bond holdings by the Federal Reserve was largely offset when $500 million worth of gold flowed out during the period of the purchase program. In addition, discounts and advances by the Federal Reserve fell by $400 million.[3] Thus, the increase in the monetary base was only a relatively modest $100 million. So the program had only one-tenth of the impact on the economy predicted by the program, but it was certainly a move in the right direction. Unfortunately, the pressure from Congress stopped when it adjourned for the summer. Within the Federal Reserve, there had been some dissent over the open market purchase program anyway, and since a unanimous decision to continue the program could not be reached, the Federal Reserve decided to halt the purchases.[4] Federal Reserve security holdings were roughly constant for the remainder of the year. In June the gold outflow was reversed, and as a result, the base continued to rise, but it was more than offset by a falling money multiplier as the public continued to increase their holdings of currency relative to bank deposits. Therefore, in spite of what appeared to be a dramatic change in Federal Reserve policy, the stock of money was still falling, although at a much slower rate than during 1931. However, the economy actually began to show a few signs of life. In July wholesale prices started to rise, as did industrial production in August. Friedman and Schwartz note that "the data . . . have many of the earmarks of a cyclical revival" (1963, 324).

8.3. The Final Wave of Bank Failures

The First National Bank of Melrose was the first to go. There was no warning; in the middle of the banking day the doors were closed by the examiners. It was one of the oldest banks in the state, regarded as a branch of the United States Treasury. Within two or three hours everyone knew of the disaster. Depositors, stunned and disbelieving, gathered in small groups to read the notice on the door . . .

There was little public lamentation. The most shocking example was old Mrs. Gearman. She beat with her fists upon the closed plate-glass doors and screamed and sobbed without restraint. She had in a savings account the $2,000 from her husband's insurance and $963 she had saved over a period of twenty-five years from making rag rugs. Nothing was left but charity.

—*An incident during the winter of 1932–33
described in Meltzer (1969, 68)*

The recovery proved to be only temporary, however, because yet another series of bank failures broke out. Bank failures had not been an especially serious problem during 1932, except for a brief spurt in June. However, in December 1932 yet another wave started, this time in the west and midwestern United States. By January 1933 the panic was spreading, and in February and March the banking system, so greatly weakened by three years of deposit withdrawals, simply collapsed. Statewide banking moratoriums were declared—several entire states were without a single operating bank during parts of February and March. Some banks just suspended operations for a period of weeks, which meant that people who had deposits were not able to withdraw them. In many other cases banks went bankrupt and people with deposits in those banks simply lost them. Vast amounts of financial wealth just disappeared off the books. The Federal Reserve Board of Governors reports that for the year 1933, 4,000 banks suspended operations, either temporarily or permanently (1943, 283). Virtually all of those suspensions occurred from January through March. Of those 4,000 banks suspending operations, 1,275 were members of the Federal Reserve system, the remainder were not. These suspended banks represented over $3.5 billion of deposits, and the Federal Reserve estimates that the actual losses to depositors from bank failures that year was $540 million. As a result, the stock of money plummeted, as did spending.[5] The unemployment rate continued to climb, reaching its twentieth-century high of 25 percent in March 1933.[6]

How could such a thing happen? Why didn't the lender of last resort try to avert this financial collapse? There appear to be a number of reasons why the Federal Reserve was dormant during the first few months of 1933. First was the fact that most of the failing banks were relatively small banks in the West and Midwest that were not members of the Federal Reserve. Since they were not members, the Federal Reserve Board felt under no obligation to help out. Second was the fact that the real bills doctrine was still in operation. While the Federal Reserve Banks could have taken U.S. Treasury securities as collateral for discounts to banks, they did not. They continued to practice the real bills doctrine, which meant that commercial paper was the eligible collateral for discounts. As pointed out earlier, the quantity of commercial paper was greatly reduced during the Depression—by 1933 there was very little available. Yet the attitude of the Federal Reserve was that a "properly managed" bank held commercial paper. No commercial paper? Then it must be a badly managed bank! So when banks were unable to come up with any commercial paper to use as collateral for discounts, the Federal Reserve's attitude was that those banks must be badly managed and, in the Darwinian scheme of things, deserved to fail.

Friedman and Schwartz make a strong case that the root of the problem was the leadership of the Federal Reserve (1963, 407–19). For example, they note that the recession of 1929–30 was no worse than the recessions of 1923–24 and 1926–27. Yet, during those earlier two recessions the Federal Reserve vigorously purchased U.S. Treasury securities in magnitudes of hundreds of millions of dollars and therefore helped keep those recessions from deepening. From 1929 to 1930, however, the Federal Reserve took no vigorous action except for the New York Federal Reserve's renegade bond purchases following the stock market crash for which they were so greatly criticized by the Federal Reserve Board in Washington. Even worse, the Federal Reserve then opened the year 1931 by selling bonds because they considered the low interest rates then prevailing to be indicative of easy credit conditions. During the waves of bank failures the leaders of the Federal Reserve seemed in over their heads, unwilling to take action, essentially at a loss about what their responsibilities were.

According to Friedman and Schwartz, the problem was the shift in leadership from the Federal Reserve Bank of New York to the Board of Governors and the other Federal Reserve District Banks. During the first several years of the Federal Reserve's existence, monetary policy and international transactions were largely carried out by the Federal Reserve Bank of New York under the leadership of Benjamin Strong. Over the years, the New York Fed became much more sophisticated about monetary matters than the other district banks, and Benjamin Strong became the major force in U.S. monetary affairs. Unfortunately, Strong passed away in October 1928. The leadership of the New York Fed passed to George Harrison, whom Friedman and Schwartz consider knowledgeable about monetary affairs, but lacking the personal force of Benjamin Strong.

In addition, shortly after Strong's death the manner in which monetary affairs were determined was changed. Previously, monetary affairs were determined by a five-person committee headed by the governor of the Federal Reserve Bank of New York. This committee evolved into a twelve-person committee of governors, most of whom resented the New York Fed's dominance of previous years. Thus, Harrison had considerably less power than Benjamin Strong had enjoyed, and when Harrison made proposals to undertake stimulative policies, he was consistently voted down by people who knew far less about monetary affairs than he. The only notable proposal by Harrison that was adopted was the open market purchase plan of 1932.

It is because of this sequence of events that Friedman and Schwartz express their view (also shared by no less than Irving Fisher and Lester Chandler) that "if Strong had still been alive and head of the New York Bank in the fall of 1930, he would very likely have recognized the oncoming liquidity crisis for what it was, would have been prepared by experience and conviction to head it off, and would have had the standing to carry the system with him" (Friedman and Schwartz 1963, 412–13). In other words, the recession that started in 1929 would likely not have been transformed into the Great Depression.[7]

8.4.   A Weak Reed to Lean On

The Federal Reserve Board in those times was a body of startling incompetence.

—*John Kenneth Galbraith (1954, 27)*

Finally, we return to Herbert Hoover. He was among those calling upon the Federal Reserve to do something positive and decisive, but they were not listening. Here is an extremely insightful exchange between President Herbert Hoover and the Federal Reserve Board that took place during late February and early March, 1933, *while the banking system was in total collapse.* This correspondence is taken from Hoover's *Memoirs* (1952, 211–12). First, Hoover's letter to the Board written on February 28:

Gentlemen:

Since my letter of a few days ago the banking situation has obviously become one of even greater gravity. I naturally wish to be properly advised as to such measures as can be taken to prevent the hardships to millions of people which are now going on. Although the Board is not the technical adviser of the President, yet it appears to me that in the large sense it should be prepared to advise me as to the measures necessary for the protection of the banking and currency system in times of emergency. I would, therefore, be glad to know whether the Board considers it desirable:

(a) To establish some form of Federal guarantee of banking deposits; or

(b) To establish clearing house systems in the affected areas; or

(c) To allow the situation to drift along under the sporadic State and community solutions now in progress ...

Very truly,

Herbert Hoover

And the Federal Reserve Board's response, dated March 2, 1933:

Dear Mr. President:

The Board has received and carefully considered your letter of February 28, 1933.

In response to your first inquiry, the Board has requested me to advise you that it is not at this time prepared to recommend any form of Federal guarantee of banking deposits ...

With respect to your second inquiry ... in reference to the establishment of clearing house systems ...

We know that the question of issuing clearing house certificates has been or is being considered in the communities ... but, for a number of reasons ... [the Board members] have not felt, up to this time, that it would be feasible or desirable for them to resort to such a device ...

Answering your third inquiry, ... so far no additional measures or authority have developed in concrete form, which at the moment, the Board feels it would be justified in urging.

Hoover wrote back to the Board:

Gentlemen ...

I am familiar with the inherent dangers in any form of federal guarantee of banking deposits, but I am wondering whether or not the situation has reached the time when the Board should give further consideration to this possibility . . .

Hoover tells us of the Board's response: "The majority of the Board again declined to have any part in the proposed recommendations . . . I concluded [that the Federal Reserve Board] was indeed a weak reed for a nation to lean on in time of trouble."

8.5. Germany: Too Little, Too Late

The situation in Germany during 1932 was a considerable improvement over the previous year. The banking situation was stabilized by a combination of bank mergers and a program carried out by both the government and the Reichsbank that involved major purchases of shares in the German banks. By 1932 the government and central bank had majority ownership of many of the country's leading banks. The point was not to control them, but to help them out financially (Hardach 1984, 227). Chancellor Bruning, who had done so much to anger the electorate and thereby raise the vote tally for the Nazis, was ousted that spring. The new chancellor, Franz von Papen, pursued expansionary monetary and fiscal policies and recovery was under way later that year. In addition, Germany received a very good piece of news during 1932: the World War I reparations were canceled at the Lausanne Conference that summer.

Unfortunately, it was too late. The National Socialists had gotten their foot in the door and during the November 1932 elections received about 44 percent of the vote. No coalition could form a majority until January 1933 when von Papen gave his support to Adolf Hitler to form a government with Hitler as chancellor and von Papen as vice chancellor. They took power in January 1933, and the rest, as they say, is history.

CHAPTER 9

Economic Recovery:
The Early Years
of the New Deal

———◦———

This great nation will endure as it has endured, will revive and will prosper. So, first of all, let me assert my firm belief that the only thing we have to fear is fear itself—nameless, unreasoning, unjustified terror which paralyzes needed efforts to convert retreat into advance.

> —*A portion of Franklin D. Roosevelt's inaugural*
> *address, delivered on Saturday, March 4, 1933*

———◦———

When the economy bottomed out in March 1933, a large segment of the American population wallowed in economic misery. The unemployment rate stood at 25 percent, output was only three-fourths of its 1929 level, and the banking system had collapsed. The picture in early 1933 looked about as grim in several other countries as well. Canada, Czechoslovakia, Germany, and Poland, as well as the United States, all suffered declines in industrial production of more than 50 percent during the period from 1929 to 1933 (Romer 1993, 22).

Yet, at the same time, there was reason for hope. In two of the countries hardest hit by the Depression, new leaders were in office. Adolf Hitler had become chancellor of Germany in January 1933, and Franklin Roosevelt was inaugurated as U.S. president in March.[1] Each had ideas about how to help promote recovery. Hitler's plan was called National Socialism while Roosevelt's was called the New Deal. Hitler's plan was successful in the sense that it helped promote a strong recovery that returned the economy back to full employment by 1937. Yet it is important to remember that this recovery coincided with a total loss of individual freedom for the German people. The New Deal's role in promoting recovery in the United States is less clear. While some argue that it was quite stimulative, more recent views suggest that parts of the program actually hindered recovery and prolonged the Depression in the United States. Yet while several of the New Deal programs were counterproductive, they were never associated with reductions in individual freedoms to the extent of those taking place in Germany at the time.

9.1.   Goals of the New Deal

The economic logic underlying the New Deal programs was in some areas sound and in other areas badly flawed. A major idea underlying many New Deal programs was the goal of stopping the deflation. Unfortunately, there was some confusion about how best to accomplish this goal. In the areas of industry and agriculture the idea was to prevent prices and wages from falling further in an effort to maintain incomes of industrial workers and farmers. This policy was counterproductive in that it hindered the natural adjustment of the economy back toward the low unemployment rates that had been attained before the Depression began. In the areas of banking and finance, however, the talk was about reflation, or driving prices back up. This goal was sound because it would be accomplished by monetary stimulus. To help bring this stimulus about, the New Deal programs attempted to reduce the role of gold, strengthen the Federal Reserve, and restore the soundness of the banking system to prevent further bank failures.

Additional goals of the New Deal were to reduce unemployment and stimulate spending. But here again, the programs were not always well thought out. Unemployment was to be reduced by work relief programs that involved the federal government hiring people to do various things. Indeed, under these programs millions of people were employed. Government employment of workers was justified as a method of stimulating spending. Workers would not only be helped by earning incomes once again, but also, in the process of spending them, these workers would raise the level of commerce and employment in general. Yet at the same time, laws were being passed that were designed to maintain or actually raise wages to levels that would clearly hinder employment in the private sector. In addition, taxes were raised, which worked to reduce spending by households. So the New Deal programs were a mixed bag; some of them worked to accomplish sound goals while others tended to hinder the recovery.

9.2. Banking and Finance

Federal insurance of bank deposits was the most important structural change in the banking system to result from the 1933 panic, and, indeed in our view the structural change most conducive to monetary stability since state bank notes were taxed out of existence immediately after the Civil War.
—*Milton Friedman and Anna J. Schwartz (1963, 434)*

Probably the best legislation that came out of the New Deal was in the area of banking and finance. Roosevelt's inauguration took place in the midst of the final wave of bank failures of the Depression period. On Inauguration Day, March 4, about half the states had already declared bank holidays. Incredibly, on that day even the Federal Reserve Banks, our lenders of last resort, joined in the holiday as they too suspended payments. Two days later, the president proclaimed a National Banking Holiday wherein all banks in the country would restrict payments. All banks were closed, and payments of cash were restricted. The idea was to allow time to restore sanity and trust in the soundness of the banks before they were allowed to reopen. Thus, irrational bank runs would be brought to a halt. In addition, Roosevelt suspended the export of gold as well as conversion of dollars for gold, which effectively removed the United States from the gold standard. He also stipulated that banks could reopen in mid-March, but only if they had been licensed and thus given the stamp of approval and soundness by the relevant banking authority. Congress backed the president by passing the Emergency Banking Act on March 9. This act gave congressional approval to Roosevelt's moves, as well as declaring gold clauses in existing contracts null and void. Gold clauses were common in contracts of the time; they obligated the debtor to pay the creditor a certain amount of gold dollars (or their equivalent in currency) of the sort that existed at the time the contract was signed.

The Roosevelt administration wanted to raise the price of gold because that would allow the existing gold stock to provide the legal backing for a larger stock of currency. However, if the U.S. government raised the price of gold when gold clauses were in effect, it would cause a massive transfer of wealth from debtors to creditors. For example, suppose someone had borrowed $100 from a bank, and the loan agreement contained a gold clause. If the price of gold were raised by 50 percent then the gold equivalent the borrower owed the bank is suddenly worth 50 percent more, so that person would owe a total of $150. Such a change in the debt on all existing contracts would amount to an enormous sum of wealth transferred from borrowers to banks and other lenders. Aside from the depressing effect upon household spending this would have, banks had enough problems reestablishing their claim to the public's trust. Therefore, it was important to get rid of the gold clauses before gold prices were raised.[2]

Before gold prices were actually raised, however, the Banking Act of 1933 (also known as the Glass-Steagall Act) was passed in June and signed by Roosevelt. This act had four major provisions. First and foremost, it established the Federal Deposit Insurance Corporation. Effective January 1, 1934, insured deposits were covered up to a maximum of $2,500. Deposit insurance is arguably the single most important change to come out of the New Deal because the United States, long plagued by waves of bank panics, saw this one stopped in its tracks and has never had another since federal deposit insurance took effect.[3]

The last three provisions of the act were based on the idea that the bank failures had resulted from cutthroat competition in banking. While this view is highly questionable, many people at the time firmly believed it to be true and concluded that the banking industry needed to be regulated more tightly. The act stipulated that Federal Reserve member banks could no longer pay interest on demand deposits (checking accounts) and that the Federal Reserve could now set the maximum interest rates payable on savings and time deposits at member banks. This interest rate regulation was extended to all insured banks two years later. The idea was to remove the temptation of banks to take great risks in order to offer the highest interest rates on deposits.

In addition, the law dictated that commercial banks could not engage in investment banking (underwriting securities) because this was considered too risky an activity.[4] Finally, the act strengthened the Federal Reserve further by establishing the Federal Open Market Committee, which was given the power to guide monetary policy. The committee would consist of the governors of the twelve Federal Reserve District Banks.[5]

The price of gold was raised the following year by the 1934 Gold Reserve Act. The official price of an ounce of gold was raised 52 percent, from $20.67 to $35.00. To help make sure the price of gold stayed at

$35.00, the law stipulated control of the market by making it illegal for U.S. citizens to hold gold except for "legitimate" purposes, such as jewelry, artwork, and industrial and scientific work. Gold certificates would no longer be redeemed for gold, all gold was nationalized, and gold coins were to be melted down and stored in the form of bullion. Finally, a fund of $2 billion was created for the U.S. Treasury to use to stabilize the value of the dollar on foreign exchange markets. In effect, the Gold Reserve Act accomplished the following: it placed the United States on a gold standard that was not really a gold standard in the traditional sense of the word. It was a gold standard only in the sense that it fixed the price of gold in terms of dollars. This, in turn, worked to help fix the exchange rate of the dollar with other currencies that were also fixed in terms of gold. Yet, this system was not a true gold standard because the Federal Reserve was not bound to allow gold flows to influence the quantity of money. The act accomplished something else too: by raising the price of gold in terms of dollars, it led to the depreciation of the dollar against other currencies. This made U.S. goods and services cheaper for foreigners to buy, which was designed to improve the U.S. net export position.

The third and final major banking and finance law passed during the New Deal was the Banking Act of 1935.[6] The basic point of this law was to centralize control of the Federal Reserve and extend its authority. The Board of Governors was established to replace the Federal Reserve Board. That the governors would run the operation was indicated by another provision of the act: heads of the twelve district banks, previously called governors, would now be called presidents. Unlike the government, in central banking a governor outranks a president. Governors were to hold staggered fourteen-year terms. Seven governors were placed on the Federal Open Market Committee along with five seats for the district bank presidents who would hold the positions on a rotating basis. The governors were also given the authority to set required reserve ratios for member banks. Yet another important feature of the 1935 law was that it allowed the Federal Reserve to discount against any security it deemed satisfactory. In effect, Congress was telling the Federal Reserve to start including U.S. Treasury securities as eligible paper and drop the real bills doctrine that had caused so much trouble from 1929 to 1933.

It is instructive to look at the patterns of the monetary base and money multiplier components during the period when these various laws were passed. Most profound, perhaps, is the obvious return of public confidence in the banking system. The best proxy for this confidence is the currency–deposit ratio, which is the amount of money people hold in the form of currency relative to bank deposits. Each run on a bank withdraws cash from the bank and thus puts currency in the hands of the public. Deposits are destroyed, so the currency–deposit ratio rises. Figure 9.1 shows that the currency–deposit ratio more than doubled between 1929 and 1933, peaking during the last bank panic, which started in December 1932 and ran through to the National Banking Holiday in March 1933. Interestingly, the public confidence returned as soon as the banks reopened; Friedman and Schwartz's data show the currency–deposit in April was below that of March (1963, 804).[7] The public did not wait until deposit insurance took effect to return their funds to the banks.

The money multiplier stabilized after the final bank crisis was over because the falling currency–deposit ratio was offset by the rising reserve–deposit ratio. The fact that the reserve—deposit ratio kept rising after the banking system had stabilized was due to increased holdings of excess reserves by banks. Friedman and Schwartz attribute the increase to the rapid gold inflows taking place at the time, which raised the level of bank reserves (1963, 518). But other factors must have been at work as well.

One likely possibility is that there were not many profitable loan opportunities available at the time. In fact, from June 30, 1933, to June 30, 1937, commercial bank loans and investments rose a total of $9.1 billion, but of that amount only $1.1 billion is accounted for by loans (Federal Reserve Board of Governors 1943, 19). If there were so few profitable loan opportunities, then why didn't the banks use the bulk of the excess reserves to buy securities? The reason is likely twofold. First, yields on short-term Treasury bills were extremely low during the period. For example, the yield on a three-month Treasury bill during July 1935 averaged .05 percent, or .0005.[8] Why bother buying Treasury bills when the yield is almost zero? A second reason may be that bankers were extremely cautious. After all, bank managers had just watched thousands of banks fail over a period of a few years and seen the Federal Reserve sit by and watch it happen. Banks could help protect themselves from another wave of panics by increasing their excess reserve position to ensure liquidity.

The behavior of the money stock is shown in figure 9.2, which shows both the stock of money (the M2 measure) and below that its growth rate in annualized terms. These figures clearly show that the stock of money stopped falling in early 1933. It then began to grow very rapidly thereafter, at double-digit rates through the mid-1930s. Since the money mul-

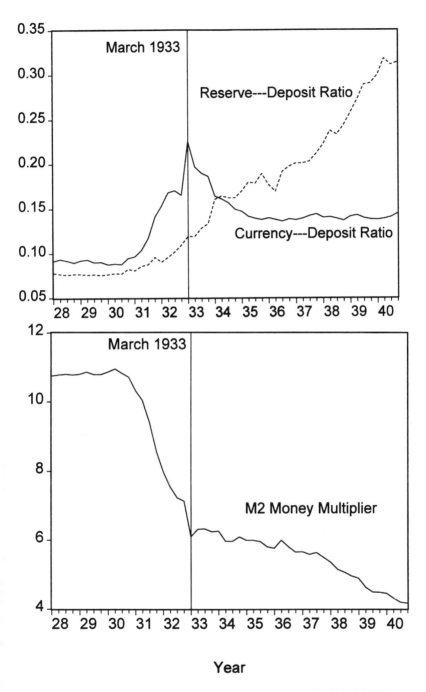

Fig. 9.1.   Confidence in the banking system returned after March 1933

tiplier was falling slowly from 1933 on, the rapid growth of money must have been the result of rapid growth of the monetary base.

The basic reason why the monetary base rose so rapidly after 1933 was the inflow of gold. In fact, the rise in the base was almost entirely due to the gold inflow because Federal Reserve credit outstanding was almost constant over the period. In other words, the rise in the base was not due to any activist policy by the Federal Reserve. Instead, it was the result of the Federal Reserve passively allowing the gold inflow to raise the base instead of sterilizing it as they had during the 1920s and early 1930s.

The value of the U.S. gold stock tripled from 1933 to 1937. This enormous rise resulted from three factors. First, raising the price of gold from $20.67 to $35.00 per ounce meant that the value of the existing gold stock was raised 52 percent. Second, with the price increase, the profitability of gold mining rose, and more gold was produced and sold in the United States and around the world. Third, an enormous amount of gold flowed into the United States because a large-scale capital flight from Europe was taking place. Many Europeans were rightly concerned about the rise of Adolf Hitler and the National Socialists in Germany, and in response they moved their financial capital to the United States, which was the safe haven of the 1930s.

Why didn't the Federal Reserve sterilize the inflow as they had during previous years? Friedman and Schwartz contend that it was the result of a combination of factors (1963, 518–19). One was that the Federal Reserve did not want to appear to be taking any actions that looked contractionary. Many members of Congress were very angry with the Federal Reserve for its inaction during the early 1930s, and there were a number of legislative proposals floating around that were considered anti–Federal Reserve.[9] Another important reason was that the district banks were concerned about their earnings. Since the revenue they use to support the operation of these banks is the interest they receive, the sale of a large amount of their U.S. government securities would reduce their revenue and earnings.

So a major monetary expansion began in 1933 that lasted until late 1936. It certainly helped promote economic recovery because it was associated with a significant rise in aggregate demand, output, and prices. The New Deal legislation had quite a bit to do with this monetary expansion because raising the price of gold had helped stimulate the gold inflow, and the advent of deposit insurance made sure that there would be no ugly repeats of the banking crises. Yet a large part of the monetary expansion resulted from a factor that certainly was not legislated in the

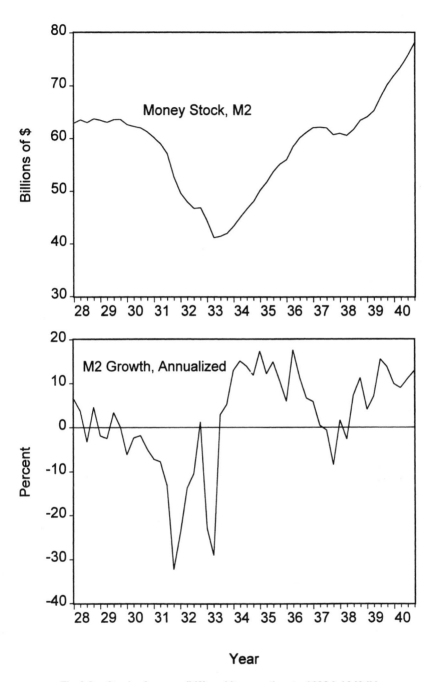

Fig. 9.2. Stock of money (M2) and its growth rate, 1928.I–1940.IV

New Deal: the rise of Adolf Hitler. The Federal Reserve, meanwhile, did little to promote this monetary expansion, unless one considers passively watching a gold inflow raise the monetary base to be an active policy to promote expansion. In fact, Friedman and Schwartz point out that discount-rate policy during the period was tight because the discount rate was well above short-term market rates (1963, 514–15).

9.3. Wages and Prices

The [National Recovery Act] was producing friction and evasion. Henry Ford was refusing to sign the codes. William Randolph Hearst . . . was proclaiming that the letters NRA stood for "No Recovery Allowed." As the various industrial codes were at last worked out and approved . . . some employers were planning to comply with their provisions fairly and honorably; others were welcoming the chance given them to gather around the table and quietly fix prices, but were resolving to evade the wage and hour clauses and to make a dead letter of Section 7a of the Recovery Act, which guaranteed collective bargaining.
—*Frederick Lewis Allen (1940, 131–32)*

The New Deal regulated business in an attempt to stimulate the economy. Unfortunately, the effort was based on convoluted logic. The Roosevelt administration felt that a major cause of the Depression was falling wages and prices. With respect to prices they may well have been right. After all, the great American economist Irving Fisher was making exactly that point at the height of the crisis (1933). He clearly believed that deflation, by raising the burden of debt, had contributed mightily to the Depression. Modern writers have made similar arguments about the period (for example, DeLong and Summers 1986). The problem with the New Deal was that the Roosevelt administration was treating the symptom of the problem as opposed to the problem itself.

The deflation had been the result of falling aggregate demand for goods and services by consumers and business; deflation was certainly exacerbating the situation, but it was not the root cause of the low output and high unemployment. The root cause was low aggregate demand. Thus, the solution to the problem was to stimulate aggregate demand to reverse the deflation. But the Roosevelt administration tried to stop the deflation by simply fixing wages and prices so they could not fall further.

For industry, this policy was carried out through the National Industrial Recovery Act of 1933 (NIRA). For agriculture it was carried out through the Agricultural Adjustment Act of 1933 (AAA).

The NIRA was one of the most controversial programs of the New Deal. It consisted of two parts, industrial regulation through the National Recovery Administration (NRA) and unemployment relief through the Public Works Administration (PWA). Much of the debate at the time revolved around the NRA, which set out to write codes for each industry that listed approved "fair trade practices" and labor standards. The writing of the codes was dominated by the industry itself and included such features as price fixing and rules against selling below cost.

In addition, the NIRA exempted industries that had agreed to the codes from the U.S. antitrust laws. In early July 1933, about three weeks after the NIRA had become law, the cotton-textile industry became the first industry to agree to codes. By the end of the month, more than 200 industry codes had been submitted, but the Roosevelt administration felt that the process was moving too slowly. In an effort to speed things up, on July 27, 1933, Roosevelt proposed blanket codes that would apply to all industries. The blanket code required employers to adhere to the following:[10]

1. do not employ anyone under 16 years of age in manufacturing
2. maximum workweek of forty hours
3. minimum wage of $12 to $15 per week for service sector office workers and salespeople, depending on size of city
4. for factory workers, a minimum wage of 40 cents per hour, or the wage in effect on July 25, 1929, but no less that 30 cents per hour
5. do not reduce existing wage rates that are currently above the code's specified minima
6. support the NRA by only dealing with other firms that are also members of the NRA
7. raise prices only by amounts necessary to cover increased costs associated with complying with the codes, or associated with increased costs incurred since July 1
8. each industry should submit its own code of fair competition as soon as possible

The basic goals of the NRA were to abolish child labor, shorten the workweek, raise wages, and control prices. The major problem was holding down the price increases. The invitation to submit codes of fair competition became a blanket invitation for industries to form cartels and raise prices. The codes were largely written by the various industry trade associations that had been formed during the 1920s at the instigation of then–Commerce Secretary Herbert Hoover (Bellush 1975, 4–5).

Handing a trade association the authority to write up a "code of fair competition" is tantamount to handing an alcoholic the key to the liquor cabinet. They can not resist the temptation to abuse the situation. The trade associations wrote up codes that raised prices, eliminated competition among the firms in the industry, and set production limits (Chandler 1970, 233–34). Within a short time, the blanket codes covered a huge proportion of industry. According to estimates provided by Chandler, 95 percent of industrial workers were covered by the codes by 1935 (1970, 230). Participating firms would display the emblem of the blue eagle to show that they were part of the NRA.

For a variety of reasons, dissatisfaction with the industrial codes was widespread by the end of 1933. One complaint was about prices; wholesale prices of nonfood items rose 12 percent during the second half of 1933, and "there can be little doubt that the codes played an important role in raising these prices" (Chandler 1970, 235). In the area of labor, one of the hopes of the supporters of the NIRA was that it would encourage unionization of industry. Section 7a of the law specified workers' right to organize and elect their own representatives to bargain collectively in their interest.

While inroads were made by unions in a few industries, for the most part unions did not gain meaningful footholds because the NRA ruled that a firm could meet the law by bargaining with a company union.[11] In addition, there were many strikes and work stoppages because of disagreements between companies and workers over wages. The NRA was shortening the workweek, and workers wanted to make sure their weekly income was not reduced because of shorter hours. Many companies felt that they should not have to pay workers the same income for less work, and there were many disagreements over this point. There were also disagreements between companies in the same industry over how the NRA codes should be interpreted with respect to labor. The result was widespread labor disruption, illustrated by the fact that from 1932 to 1933 the number of man-days of labor lost due to strikes and lockouts more than doubled to 14.8 million (Hacker 1934, 120).

By early 1935 the problems with the NRA were coming to a head. The work stoppages continued as a result of labor's dissatisfaction with the program. Managers of firms in the same industry were in disagreement because, as with any cartel, cheating on the agreements became widespread. The NRA faced widespread noncompliance with the codes. In addition, the public was dissatisfied with the codes because of the price increases and monopolistic practices. The great experiment in industrial planning finally came to an end in May 1935, when the Supreme Court ruled that the NIRA was unconstitutional. Yet, although the NIRA was dead, many facets of the program were resurrected under plans that followed. These are described in chapter 11.[12]

By 1933, the economy's agricultural sector was in dire straits. The major declines in agricultural prices from 1929 to 1933 had been an absolute disaster for farmers. Farm prices fell over 50 percent from 1929 to 1933, and farm per-capita income is estimated to have fallen by two-thirds over that same period (Hughes 1987, 455). During the worst year, 1933, about one out of every twenty U.S. farms either defaulted on its debts or entered into a forced sale (Soule 1947, 444).

The Roosevelt administration's attempt to aid the farm sector was carried out through the Agricultural Adjustment Act of 1933. The act's goal was quite simple: to raise farm incomes. To achieve this goal, the law did what had been done in industry through the NRA: interfere with the market and legislate prices. The AAA set up a complicated system to raise prices of seven major farm products through allotments that would control output.[13] Eight more products were added to the allotment system over the next two years. Under this system, farmers were allocated output quotas. Farmers who entered into the agreements to control output also received a government subsidy payment as an inducement to join the program. In addition, the Secretary of Agriculture was empowered to set up agreements between farmers, processors, and distributors of agricultural products that would include marketing quotas and price fixing. These agreements were to be exempt from the antitrust laws.

While it is not clear how much of the price increase was due to the new law, there is no doubt that farm income rose following passage of the AAA. Farm income, which bottomed out in 1932 at $1.93 billion, rose dramatically through to 1937 when it stood at $5.23 billion (Chandler 1970, 217). By 1937, the default and forced-sale rate for farms was less than half of what it had been in 1933 (Soule 1947, 444). Yet it is not clear how much of the improvement in farming was the result of the AAA because the drought that generated the dust bowl became acute in 1934 and was at its worst in 1936. Output of several farm products, especially those grown in the Great Plains sections of the United States and Canada, fell dramatically. Given the inelastic demand for agricultural products, drought-induced reductions in supply generated significant price increases for farm products.

Therefore, in both agriculture and industry, the Roosevelt administration set up a system with the intent to raise prices and reduce output. In industry, it was to be accomplished through the formation of cartels, in agriculture through price fixing and output restrictions. The macroeconomic effect of these programs can be seen by the behavior of output and prices during 1934. From 1933 to 1934, aggregate demand rose 16.5 percent. Of that amount, 7.4 percent can be attributed to increasing output, and the remaining 9.1 percent was increasing prices. Given the vast amount of excess capacity in the economy during 1934, it seems hardly possible that more than half the demand growth would show up in prices in the absence of the NRA and AAA. Had the NRA and AAA not been established, a much greater proportion of demand growth would certainly have shown up in increasing output instead of prices. In other words, the combination of cartels, wage hikes, and regulation of agriculture brought about by the New Deal surely hindered the recovery.[14]

9.4. Relief for the Impoverished

They were a gentle-faced old man, with tears rolling down from his cheeks, and a young woman sobbing quietly with her head on his shoulder . . . The old man's wife had died the day before . . . the young woman was his married daughter from Detroit. . . . "What's going to become of him now?" she burst out between her sobs. "I can't take him back with me. I can't, I tell you! My husband has only two days' work a week, and we have children. We're almost starving ourselves, and he would have to starve with us. I had to borrow from all the neighbors—a dollar here and a dollar there—to get the money to come up here. And the little bit of insurance Mother had will only pay to bury her. Please help him! You can't let my old father starve!"

"Of course we won't let him starve," I said. "We're going to take care of him. That's what we are here for—to see that people like your father don't suffer in any way which we can prevent . . .

The city case-worker called on them in about an hour. She found the usual pathetic scene, which we afterwards saw so often. The dead wife and mother lay in her coffin in the shabby little parlor. That case-worker, with her calm, kind manner, was just the one to comfort them. The father became one of our regular direct relief cases, and he was one of the most lovable of all our old men.

> —*Louise Armstrong (1938, 85–86), who with her husband left Chicago after the panic and moved to rural northern Michigan. There, she worked as a District Administrator for the Federal Emergency Relief Administration (FERA).*

The New Deal directly dealt with impoverished people through relief payments. This relief took two forms: direct relief and public works. Direct relief was direct transfer payments to the unemployed while public works represented government employment for wages.

Direct relief payments were made by state and local governments, partly funded by the federal government. When the federal government decided to make relief payments to the impoverished, officials realized that the most efficient way to accomplish this was to work through the state and local relief agencies that were already in place. It was much easier to work through those agencies rather than set up an entire new layer of bureaucracy to administer relief. As a result, the federal government, through the Federal Emergency Relief Administration (FERA) that was established in 1933, greatly increased grants-in-aid to state and local governments from 1933 to 1935. Federal grants-in-aid to state and local governments, which had been $134 million during 1932, rose to $1.7 billion by 1935 (Chandler 1970, 192). During 1934, an estimated one-sixth of American families were receiving relief payments (Soule 1947, 315). While the amounts actually paid to individuals were relatively small, averaging $6.50 per week, at least it was something (Leuchtenburg 1963, 123). An average working person's wage at the time was around $15 to $20 per week.

Work relief was carried out through several agencies, including the Civilian Conservation Corps (CCC), Civil Works Administration (CWA), Public Works Administration (PWA), and Works Progress Administration (WPA). These agencies employed people to do a wide variety of things, including building roads, dams, and buildings; improving harbors; and making improvements in national parks. Funding was also provided to build naval ships. In addition, artists, writers, and musicians were supported in their work.

The wages paid were not high, in fact in the beginning a relief worker did not earn enough to raise their income above a poverty level, although the incomes of two workers would lift a family above the poverty line. The programs did, however, employ millions of people and spend significant amounts of funds doing so. By 1934, the peak year of federal employment, over four million people were employed in these programs and paid total wages of over $1.5 billion. Combined with the direct relief payments, by the end of 1934 the New Deal had spent nearly $3.5 billion (Campagna 1987, 126). This is a significant amount when you consider that 1934 GNP was $65.3 billion.[15]

As a result, there is little doubt that the relief programs were expansionary during 1933 and 1934 and thereby aided the recovery. However, some of the potential gains were squandered because of the tax hikes taking place at the time. The 1932 tax hike sponsored by Hoover was having its full effect during 1933, enough so that Brown estimates that federal fiscal policy was more contractionary during 1933 than in 1932 (Brown 1956). Then, during 1933, the Roosevelt Administration supported the first in a series of antibusiness tax laws that were passed during the 1930s.

Tax increases were enacted during the 1930s because the Roosevelt Administration followed the same logic on the federal budget that Hoover had followed: the budget should be balanced, and the way to accomplish that was to raise taxes. The tax hikes during the period were antibusiness largely because there was a strong antibusiness feeling among the population at the time. Corporate managers had been the heroes of the 1920s, but they were the villains of the 1930s. So the tax hikes were focused on business and upper-income households. The tax changes enacted during 1933 included a 50 percent tax on corporate retained earnings, a 5 percent tax on dividend income, an increased excise tax on gasoline, a tax on corporate capital of $1 per $1,000 value of capital, and an "excess profits" tax of 5 percent on all profits over 12.5 percent of the value of the corporation's capital stock. In addition, the AAA included various taxes on processing food products produced in excess of the allocated amount. Various import tariffs were also approved. In addition, when prohibition of alcoholic beverages was repealed in December 1933, a federal excise tax was promptly imposed on those goods (Campagna 1987, 133).

In 1934 another tax hike was passed. This one, titled the Revenue Act, made the income tax more progressive. The act imposed a flat rate of 4 percent with an additional 1 percent on incomes over $4,000 to $6,000, and a tax rate of 59 percent on incomes over $1 million. In addition, it included an earned income credit so that the effective tax rate for low-income people was below the stated rates, and it included the provision that the capital gains on assets held for long durations be taxed at lower rates than those held for shorter terms (Campagna 1987, 134).

The net result was that federal fiscal policy, while more expansionary during 1934 than in 1933 thanks to the federal relief programs, could have been more expansionary and the economic recovery more vibrant than actually occurred. The combination of the upward pressure placed on wages and prices through the NRA, higher food prices from both the dust-bowl drought and the AAA, and the tax hikes enacted in 1932, 1933, and 1934 surely offset a considerable amount of the expansionary effect from the relief programs and the monetary expansion brought about by the departure from the gold standard and the gold inflows.

When judged by gains in economic output during the early years of the New Deal, the recovery started out strong but lost momentum quickly. The Federal Reserve's index of industrial production bottomed out at 59 in March 1933 and had risen to 100 by August, a very large gain over so brief a period. Then production began to falter as firms discovered they had overbuilt inventories. The index started falling and stood at 72 by November. Because this decline in production coincided with the establishment of the NRA, business and the public began to seriously question the New Deal. This marked the end of the Roosevelt administration's honeymoon period (Allen 1940, 131). The seesaw pattern of production continued during 1934. Here are the annualized quarterly growth rates of real GNP for 1933 and 1934:

1933.I	−24.0 %
1933.II	27.8 %
1933.III	30.6 %
1933.IV	−29.2 %
1934.I	21.5 %
1934.II	22.3 %
1934.III	−17.4 %
1934.IV	−0.1 %

Source: Balke and Gordon 1986

The average unemployment rate during 1933 was 25 percent. It fell to only 22.0 percent during 1934. Many indicators suggested the recovery was weak.

As a result of the weak recovery and dissatisfaction over several aspects of the New Deal, Roosevelt was being criticized from all sides. The political right was outraged by the government intrusion into the private sector of the economy. The political left was angry that the New Deal programs were not radical enough. By spring 1935, when the backbone of the program, the NRA, was held unconstitutional by the Supreme Court, the New Deal was falling apart. That same month, the U.S. Chamber of Commerce began to criticize the New Deal, indicating business's abandonment of support. Roosevelt was watching the coalition he had put together to win the 1932 election break into pieces. He knew that if he was going to retain power, something had to be done. In response, he launched the second New Deal.

CHAPTER 10

Germany: Recovery, but at a Very High Cost

━━━━►‹○‹«━━━━

Work for all, not wealth for all.
> —*A Nazi slogan in 1933, after they had abolished the*
> *labor unions (Alfred Sohn-Rethel 1978, 38–39)*

━━━━►‹○‹«━━━━

The problem facing Germany during the early 1930s was the same one the United States was trying to deal with: massive unemployment. Although the German economy had actually begun to recover somewhat during 1932, there was still a huge unemployment problem when Hitler became chancellor in January 1933. He began to assert himself in March 1933 when the German Parliament, in the wake of hysteria following the burning of the Reichstag (the parliamentary building in Berlin), passed the Enabling Act that gave Hitler dictatorial powers. With this absolute power he was able to deal with both the economy and his opposition on his own terms.[1]

Hitler's National Socialist economic system was capitalist in the sense that private ownership was maintained. Firms continued to be privately owned, as were farms. Yet the system was socialistic in the sense that owners had very little control over their economic decisions. The Nazis heavily regulated both agriculture and industry to the point of dictating prices and controlling distribution through the formation of cartels run by the government.

In the economic arena the Nazis had three primary goals: reduce unemployment, achieve self-sufficiency (autarky), and militarize in preparation for an invasion of eastern Europe. They used their system of economic controls to attempt to accomplish these goals, but with varying degrees of success.

10.1. Unemployment Policy

[On May 1, 1933] Hitler . . . declared that day's motto, "Honor work and respect the worker." Early the next morning the SA and SS struck. They occupied union offices all over Germany, confiscated funds, and jailed labor leaders . . . Before the end of the month, Hitler effectively abolished collective bargaining by putting all matters concerning wages and working conditions in the hands of government-appointed labor trustees. All trade unions were dissolved and their members transferred to the German Labor Front, under the leadership of the longtime drunkard and Nazi gauleiter [district leader] in Cologne, Robert Ley.
—*Robert Edwin Herzstein et al. (1980, 166)*

Unemployment was dramatically reduced between 1933 and 1937. At Germany's economic trough in 1932 approximately 6 million people were registered as unemployed, and according to several writers the true number was probably closer to 8 million.[2] These figures translate into an astounding unemployment rate in the neighborhood of 33 percent. By 1937 full employment had been achieved, with only around 500,000 registered unemployed, and by 1938 there was a labor shortage with just 164,000 registered unemployed (Stolper 1940, 240–41). So in terms of reducing unemployment, the Nazi economic program was remarkably successful. This incredible reduction in unemployment was brought about by a combination of (1) a massive public works program financed partly by money creation, (2) inducing women to leave the labor force, (3) drafting young men into the army, and (4) cutting out of the labor force an unknown number of "undesirables," such as Marxists and Jews, by forcing them to flee the country or interning them in concentration camps.

  1. The public works programs consisted of hiring large numbers of people to work on construction projects. According to Overy, 660,000 workers were employed in construction during 1933, and the number rose to 2 million by 1936 (1982, 50). Much of this construction was on the improved road system (autobahn), electrification projects, and hous-

ing construction. The projects were deliberately made labor intensive so as to employ more workers. Wages were low, and in some areas working conditions were poor. The road-building workers apparently had an especially bad situation with extremely poor housing and working conditions. In fact, there were incidents where the military had to break up riots by dissatisfied workers (James 1986, 304). Supposedly, these problems lessened when housing conditions were later improved (Roberts 1937, 238).

The role of the government and investment projects in the economic recovery can be seen through the proportion of output attributable to these sectors. During 1932 government purchases accounted for 17 percent of GNP, and by 1938 they accounted for 33 percent of output, which was a 300 percent increase in government purchases over that period. Also, over the period 1933 to 1938 the government was funding 45 percent of all investment in the economy (Overy 1982, 35).

This expanding public expenditure was largely financed through borrowing that was in part indirectly funded through money creation. The constitution forbade the Reichsbank from discounting (or buying) government debt, which leads to the creation of money. This was a change enacted in response to the terrible hyperinflation of 1923, which was a direct result of rapid expansion of the money stock. In the early days of the Nazi rule, new debt instruments were created to get around the restriction. The most important of these for funding public works projects were Work Creation Bills.[3] These were used in the following way: government agencies would be formed to undertake construction projects that they would then contract out to private firms. The contractor would then write out a bill of exchange for the project that obligated the agency to pay the contractor when the project was completed. The agency would sign the bill, which the contractor could then take to a bank that would accept them. The bank could then use the bill as collateral against discounts from the Reichsbank. In this way the bills ended up being monetized, or transformed into new money (Nathan 1944, 282). In addition, the money supply rose because in October 1933 the Nazis freed the Reichsbank from any restrictions by decreeing that they could conduct open market operations at their discretion and that they no longer were required to hold a 40 percent gold backing against outstanding currency. As a result, the stock of money in Germany rose nearly 60 percent from 1932 to 1938 (Overy 1982, 46).

2.   The Nazis also provided incentives for women to leave the labor force as a way to alleviate the unemployment problem. The Nazis

thought that women should be at home, producing large numbers of blue-eyed, blond, racially pure Germanic children for the good of the fatherland. To help further this goal, they set up a series of tax incentives for women to behave in this desired manner. During 1934 a law was instituted that reduced income and wage taxes for families with children. Another 1934 law provided marriage loans, whereby prospective new families could receive a grant toward the purchase of furniture and household goods. One-fourth of the debt would be forgiven for each child produced by the marriage. In addition, civil servants received a bonus for every new baby born, and there was a 15 percent income tax reduction for every child. Finally, a new law was written into the penal code that, among other things, prohibited abortion and imposed penalties for "anybody who sneers at motherhood in word or writing" (Roberts 1937, 232). These various incentives for women to leave the labor force were apparently effective: Roberts provides figures showing that an estimated 500,000 women left the labor force as a result of these laws (1937, 169).[4]

3.   The unemployment problem was also alleviated when military conscription was introduced in March 1935 as part of the militarization program discussed below. About one million young men were removed from the labor force in this way. In addition, over a million more workers were employed in running the National Socialist bureaucracy: working for the various police agencies and party offices, and serving as the officials necessary for running a tightly regulated, police-state society.

4.   Finally, the unemployment problem was further alleviated by forcibly removing a large number of people from the labor force. The actual number of "undesirables" who were placed in concentration camps or fled the country in fear is not known, but it was surely sizable. For example, Roberts reports that there were about 600,000 Jews living in Germany when the National Socialists rose to power (1937, 261). About a decade later virtually all of those people had either fled the country, were in concentration camps, or were dead. An unknown number of Marxists, Freemasons, and Gypsies met similar fates.

While unemployment clearly declined, it is not clear that the average German's standard of living was rising as significantly as might be expected. A major reason for this, quite aside from the fear of the police state and the loss of political freedom, was that the Nazis had a policy of keeping wages low and stable. When the Nazis destroyed organized labor and replaced it with their own National Labor Front in May 1933, workers immediately lost their bargaining power. Workers were now "represented" by state-appointed Trustees of Labor whose job was to make sure that wages were fixed at low rates. The trustees planted spies in workplaces who would report any workers voicing dissatisfaction or attempting to organize other workers. If someone voiced criticism over their wages or working conditions they could be thrown into a concentration camp. All this was compliments of the Nazis, whose official name was National Socialist German Workers' Party.

Since the aggregate economy was expanding rapidly while wages were stagnant, labor's share of national income was declining. Figures cited by Nathan show that labor's share of national income fell from 56.9 percent in 1932 to 53.6 percent in 1938 (1944, 338). Most of that decline is accounted for by an increase in corporate profits' share, which rose from 15.5 to 18.6 percent over that same period. These changes occurred as a deliberate goal of the Nazis: keep wages low to hold down labor costs. As a result employment would expand more rapidly than it otherwise would, and the industrialists who had financially supported Hitler's rise to power would benefit with higher profitability (Sohn-Rethel 1978, 91).

The low labor costs are illustrated by real wage data that, depending on the source, show that real wages either fell or perhaps even rose slightly.[5] In other words, if the typical German family's economic situation was improving, it was not because of rising wage rates, but rather because more members of the family were working. In addition, there is evidence that the standard of living for the average German was actually lower in the fully employed economy of 1937 than during the late 1920s before the Depression began. For example, Overy reports data that suggest that the household consumption of inferior food products such as potatoes, rye bread, and cheese was higher in 1937 than in 1927, while consumption of more desirable goods such as wheat bread, meat, fruit, and beer fell over that time span (1982, 60). Robert describes the widespread use of inferior substitute products in use at the time (1941, 38). For example, women's dresses could not contain any more than 30 percent of either silk or wool. Cellulose was mixed in as a filler.

In sum, it is undeniable that the economic recovery engineered by the National Socialists was successful in the sense of moving the economy toward full employment quickly. But that success is dampened by the fact that as Germany moved toward full employment, the workers were not receiving the entire fruits of their labor. Wages were being deliberately held down, and, as a result, the average German may have been worse off economically in the full employment economy of 1937 than he or she had been in the late 1920s. In addition, these people were undeniably worse off in terms of their personal freedom. They lived in a police state operated through terror in which anything a person said or did had the potential to land them in a concentration camp run by the worst people imaginable. It was certainly a high price to pay for full employment.

10.2. Autarky

Agriculture was the rubbish-dump of fascist industrial policies; the wrecks caused by the antagonism of its leaders reached the agrarian backdoor with the appearance of accidental stupidities to be blamed on some clumsy oaf!

—*Alfred Sohn-Rethel (1978, 74)*

The prevailing wisdom among Germans was that the Allied blockade during World War I was a major reason why Germany had lost that war. Since Hitler fully intended to be engaged in a major war in the not-too-distant future, it was important that his country not be vulnerable to another blockade. Therefore, a major goal of the National Socialists was that Germany have a self-sufficient economy. The Nazis undertook policies to attempt to achieve this goal. They established the Food Estate in an attempt to be self-sufficient in food, erected major trade barriers to prevent imports, and ordered several firms to work on developing synthetic products. The results were not particularly successful, especially in agriculture where the Food Estate was a disaster.

According to Sohn-Rethel (1978), the background to businesses' support of the autarky movement lies in the workings of three important economic interest groups that existed at the end of the 1920s. One was the landed aristocracy, referred to as the Junkers, who were centered in Prussia. Next were the steel and iron producers, whom Sohn-Rethel calls the industrialists. Last were the manufacturers, the producers of durable goods such as electrical equipment, radios, optical equipment, and scientific equipment. This latter group was violently opposed to Hitler because of his policy of autarky. These manufacturers were highly competitive in world markets in which German products were considered to be of high quality and technologically advanced. An autarky economy was very much against this group's interests because if German trade dried up these firms would lose a major proportion of their sales. The Junkers and industrialists, however, were very much interested in a self-sufficient economy because both wanted to be protected by trade barriers. The agriculture sector wanted trade barriers to keep out imports, while the iron and steel producers wanted them because their products were not especially competitive on world markets. In addition, iron and steel production had boomed during the World War I period, and business had never recovered to those levels. The agricultural and industrial interests provided financial support during Hitler's rise to power because the autarky goal, with its corresponding trade barriers, was in their interests.

In agriculture the Nazis attempted to achieve the autarky goal through an agency they created in 1933 called the Reich Food Estate. This agency set up a complicated system of controls that determined prices, profit margins, distribution, and output.[6] Every agriculture product was controlled by the Food Estate. Prices were held stable because increases would dramatically reduce the real purchasing power of urban workers whose wages were being controlled.

At the same time the Food Estate was being set up, Germany severely restricted food imports and exports, all in the name of self-sufficiency. This created problems because Germany historically was a net importer of dairy products, vegetable oils, vegetables, and animal fodder (Nathan 1944, 84). According to Sohn-Rethel (1978, 75–77), Walter Darre, the "brains" behind the operation who was in charge of the Food Estate, was such a fool that he never realized that the import restrictions would cause the country to eventually reduce its inventories of these goods down to zero. This finally happened in 1935. By 1936 a general shortage of food products existed. Officers of the expanding German army were especially angry about it. Meanwhile, the agriculture situation was further worsened by a law enacted in September 1933 titled the Hereditary Farm Law. This law decreed that farms were to be inherited by a single heir, typically the oldest son, and any other children would not share in the inheritance. The purpose of the legislation was to stop the practice of one child mortgaging the farm as a way to retain possession of the farm while distributing the family inheritance to the other children. This practice had resulted in a great deal of mortgage debt in the agriculture sector. This law had a very important unintended effect: it caused a widespread migration of disinherited children from the farms to the urban areas. This loss of farm labor combined with the inability to obtain mortgage credit has been blamed for falling output in German agriculture during the 1930s (Sohn-Rethel 1978, 72–74). The sum total of this policy was to make Germany more dependent on external agricultural products, quite the opposite effect of what had been intended.

Industrial control was carried out through the Department of Economics. Cartel arrangements had a long history in Germany, and the department was supposed to intensify the formation of cartels. The Department of Economics was empowered to form industry cartels where deemed necessary, and it had the authority to require firms to join the cartels. The department, of course, also controlled the cartels through an extremely complicated system. A strict system of price controls existed with the explicit threat of the concentration camp for those who violated them.[7] The cartel system was largely set up so as to move the economy toward a militarization program. Among other things, the Department of Economics determined which raw materials were "vital" and which were "nonvital" (Stolper 1940, 249).

The Department of Economics also tried to advance the autarky movement by requiring firms to work on developing synthetic products that could not be produced domestically. Germany is not a particularly resource-rich country, especially as far as oil and rubber are concerned. These would be extremely important materials when the war came, and Hitler did not want to be dependent on foreign countries for these goods. Most of the efforts went toward developing synthetic oil, wool, and rubber.[8] There was some success, although the costs were very high. For example, the artificial rubber cost seven times as much as natural rubber (Stolper 1940, 251). Roberts reports that it was a "deplorable sight in Germany to see a row of cheap German hats (made of artificial wool) after rain" (1937, 174).

In sum then, the autarky movement forced upon the German economy by the National Socialists was not particularly successful in removing the German economy from international dependence. It resulted in food shortages that required increased imports of certain food products. Also, Germany had to continue importing most of the necessary raw materials from neighboring countries, so the Nazi ideal of a self-sufficient economy was not achieved. When the war came Germany filled its needs by taking what it wanted from the conquered countries.

10.3. Militarization

"Gentlemen, you have put before the Reichs Government a total armaments programme costing some 21 billion RM [reichsmarks]. I have to tell you, as responsible Head of Government, that I cannot consent to an arms programme of such proportions." A pause ensued in which the icy silence froze below zero.

And then, in his most dramatic "Hitler" crescendo: "Gentlemen, I can only consent to an arms programme costing at least 35 billion RM!"

—Adolf Hitler, speaking to the assembled chiefs of the various branches of the German military on February 2, 1934 (taken from Sohn-Rethel 1978, 143–44)

One of the themes Adolf Hitler developed in his speeches was Germany's need for "breathing room" (*lebensraum,* literally "room to live"). He viewed Germany as a locked-in country with a relatively large population given its land mass. In addition, it is located near France and Russia, two of the countries it had fought against during World War I. In order to obtain this "breathing room," he intended to attack to the east and seize the vast agricultural region of Ukraine, Belarus, and western Russia, at that time all part of the Soviet Union. This attack was decided upon in 1935 and originally planned for 1939 (Sohn-Rethel 1978, 109).[9] A war on this scale would require a large quantity of military supplies and the ability to produce a great many more.

Officials in their expansive moments readily agreed that the network of roads had a military significance. "We are not building roads just for airplanes to look at," one man said. "Of course they can rush military supplies and troops to the frontiers in time of need. In fact," he went on, "you can learn a lot about German foreign policy by simply looking at the map and seeing which roads have been completed first."

—A German official discussing the new autobahn system being constructed in Germany (taken from Roberts 1937, 239). The first roads built led to the German borders with Holland, Poland, and Austria.

The militarization program fit together nicely with the plan to reduce unemployment. While many writers suggest that the militarization program did not really begin in earnest until 1937, this is not the case. The early public works projects, in particular the autobahn system, were part of the preliminary stages of militarization. The idea was that Germany would need good roads to transport the military equipment that would be built later. So while the official figures show that spending on the military did not escalate dramatically until the mid-1930s, in fact much of the early construction spending was for building the infrastructure that the military would use later.

The militarization program became official in 1935 when military conscription was instituted and Germany made it clear to the world that they no longer considered valid the restrictions on the size of their military dictated by the Treaty of Versailles. Government expenditures for rearmament, which had been 700 million RM in 1932, were 5.4 billion RM in 1935 and 10.2 billion RM in 1936 (Overy 1982, 50). Military spending in 1932 was 1.3 percent of GNP; by 1935 it was 18 percent of GNP (Overy 1982, 47). The big drive for militarization generated labor shortages by 1938.

In sum, then, the National Socialist economic recovery during the 1930s was a roaring success at reducing unemployment. In fact, some prominent Americans, notably Henry Ford and Charles Lindbergh, expressed their admiration for the German economic recovery, and in some circles Hitler was hailed as a hero for what had been accomplished. This economic recovery was brought about by highly expansionary monetary and fiscal policies that resulted in a significant increase in aggregate demand. Output rose dramatically, and the unemployment rate plummeted. From 1932 to 1938 production rose 75 percent, while production of investment goods rose 109 percent. Yet production of consumption goods rose only 32 percent, further evidence that German households were not receiving the full share of their labor (Overy 1982, 31). Inflation was never a problem for the simple reason that wage and price controls existed with the death penalty for those who avoided them. Instead, there were widespread shortages, as so often happens when wage and price controls are in force. The German public was certainly better off than they had been during the dark days of 1932 in that they had jobs and no longer had to worry about where the next meal would come from. So in that sense the Nazi economic recovery had succeeded. Yet it had come at a very high cost in that the personal freedom of the typical German was being denied to an extent that is almost unimaginable to a resident of a country like the United States.

CHAPTER 11

The Second New Deal
and the
1937–38 Recession

By 1935 the U.S. economy was far from producing at full employment. The unemployment rate averaged 20.3 percent during the year, and according to Gordon's estimates output was only 73 percent of capacity (1993). As noted in chapter 9, by early 1935 the economy's poor performance was causing Roosevelt's coalition of labor, farmers, and business to fall apart. Many blamed the New Deal programs for the weak U.S. economic recovery. Much of this wrath was focused on the NRA, which was considered an absolute, unadulterated failure by various groups, although for different reasons. Consumers were angry about the price increases, labor about the interpretation of Section 7a, and business groups were arguing about the widespread violations of the codes. A great many people cheered when the Supreme Court put the NRA out of its misery by declaring it unconstitutional in May 1935. Roosevelt was losing political support, and he was due to come up for reelection in 1936. He felt that something needed to be done.

Roosevelt's response was to launch the second New Deal in the late spring of 1935. During that year and the one that followed, a series of major laws were passed and signed by Roosevelt: the National Labor Relations Act, the Social Security Act, the Revenue Acts of 1935 and 1936, and the Banking Act of 1935.[1] These laws were important because they greatly strengthened labor unions, raised taxes, and are also blamed for further hindering the recovery.

11.1. Labor

The workers were in an explosive mood. The NRA, they said, had proved the National-Run-Around as far as they were concerned. By 1935 more than 600 federal locals had been disbanded in disgust.

—*R. O. Boyer and H. M. Morais (1970, 291)*

In plant after plant the men abruptly sat down—in the Cleveland Fisher Body plant, in Fisher Body No. 1 and Fisher Body No. 2 at Flint, in the Fleetwood and Cadillac plants at Detroit, and elsewhere. They kept enough men inside each factory to hold it as a fortress, and while these men idled, played cards, and stood guard at doors and windows, food was sent in to them from union kitchens outside. Thus began one of the most gigantic industrial conflicts in American history.

—*Frederick Lewis Allen describing the start of the United Auto Workers sit-down strike in December 1936 (1940, 230). Forty-four days later the governor of Michigan announced that General Motors had accepted the UAW as the collective bargaining agent for their employees. Remarkably, there was very little violence associated with this strike.*

Labor interests felt badly cheated by the NRA and its infamous Section 7a. When the NRA was passed, organized labor thought they were getting their big chance to strengthen labor unions because Section 7a guaranteed labor's right to bargain collectively. Labor interests were grossly disappointed over the interpretation of that section because the National Recovery Administration allowed unions controlled by the companies to bargain on behalf of employees. As a result, organized labor did not benefit in any meaningful way.

The National Labor Relations Act of 1935 represented the Roosevelt administration's attempt to win back the support of labor. This act, better known as the Wagner Act, was probably the greatest victory ever for organized labor in the United States. It established the National Labor Relations Board (NLRB) that was to guarantee workers the right to bargain collectively. Workers could sign cards stating that they wanted to be represented by a union. If a majority of workers at a firm signed the cards, an election, monitored by the NLRB, would be held to determine if a union would represent the workers. If a majority of workers voted in favor of a particular union to represent them, then that union would have the authority to bargain collectively with the employer. At the same time, the law prohibited child labor, imposed a minimum wage, and disallowed several "unfair labor practices" by both companies and unions. Among these, the stipulation that the company could not discriminate in the workplace against union members was especially important. This was a law with real teeth that clearly tilted the balance in favor of unions.

However, companies largely ignored the Wagner Act because there was a widespread belief that it would be held unconstitutional by the Supreme Court just as the NRA had been earlier. From 1935 to 1937 workers would vote for union representation only to see the company refuse to bargain collectively with the workers' bargaining unit. The ongoing labor unrest associated with strikes over union representation continued. There were several violent strikes during this period, including a disastrous episode in U.S. labor history: the Memorial Day Massacre outside a Republic Steel Plant in Chicago that left ten workers dead and many more seriously wounded. According to testimony before a congressional committee investigating the incident, the steel companies had prepared for the strike by "spending $43,901.88 . . . for machine guns, revolvers, tear gas, and bombs" (Boyer and Morais 1970, 313).

To the shock of the business world, the Wagner Act was held to be constitutional in the spring of 1937 by a 5–4 vote of the Supreme Court. Once that hurdle was passed, unionization gathered momentum. During 1933, 11.5 percent of nonagricultural workers were in unions, and by 1939 28.9 percent were (Reynolds et al. 1991, 336). Total union membership tripled over that same period.[2]

In sum, once the Wagner Act was upheld by the Supreme Court the position of organized labor improved a great deal in the United States. The first two years under the Wagner Act were characterized by a large number of work stoppages, strikes, and labor violence. Yet, from 1937 to 1939 the tide shifted, and unions gained major footholds in the American economy without a great deal of violence. In terms of the economic recovery, it is hard to quantify the impact of the Wagner Act, but a few comments can be made. First, it likely placed upward pressure on wages.[3] Vedder and Gallaway argue that the act significantly raised the wage differential between unionized and nonunionized workers (1993, 139–40). When the act was passed in 1935, unionized workers earned about 2 percent more than nonunion workers. By 1939 the differential was around 10 percent, and by 1941 it was over 23 percent. As a result, there can be little doubt that employment growth suffered in unionized industries. Vedder and Gallaway also present estimates suggesting that the growth of unions resulted in an unemployment rate 6.28 percentage points higher than would have been the case if unions had not grown so rapidly (1993, 141). In a study of ten industries, Bernanke reports that the growth of union membership under the Wagner Act resulted in a 10 percent increase in weekly earnings in six of the industries he studied (1986). These estimates are also consistent with the analysis of Gordon, who applies an insider–outsider model to explain the persistence of high unemployment during the late 1930s (Gordon 1988). By encouraging unionization, the Wagner Act raised the number of insiders (those with jobs) who had the incentive and ability to exclude outsiders (those without jobs). Once high wages have been negotiated, employers are less likely to hire outsiders, and thus the insiders could protect their own interests.[4] Second, the growth of unions afforded a much greater number of workers a sense of job security. Prior to the rise of unions, people often went to factories not knowing whether or not they would be hired that day. Sometimes they would; other days they might not be. Their employment was subject to the whims of the foreman responsible for hiring that day's labor. Unions changed that; employees who were members of unions could go to work each day knowing that they had a job. In this way unions greatly improved the typical worker's situation in life.

11.2.   Social Security

Those [social security] taxes were never a problem of economics. They are politics all the way through. We put those payroll contributions there so as to give the contributors a legal, moral and political right to collect their pensions and their unemployment benefits. With those taxes in there, no damn politician can ever scrap my social security system.

> —*Franklin D. Roosevelt (taken from Campagna 1987,*
> *122), explaining why employee withholding taxes were*
> *included. It certainly turned out to be a prescient*
> *comment, and it also demonstrates how*
> *he was a master politician.*

In 1935 the federal government entered the old-age insurance business by passing the Social Security Act. It imposed a payroll tax, collected from the employer, equal to 1 percent each from both employee and employer starting in 1937 and rising a percentage point a year to 3 percent from both employee and employer by 1939.The tax applied to the first $3,000 of income. The law exempted many categories of workers including government employees, farm workers, domestic service workers, and casual labor. The payers would receive benefit checks when they turned 65 years old. The law also included unemployment insurance. Employers were to pay 3 percent of a worker's salary into an unemployment insurance fund. The law allowed a 90 percent credit if the firm paid it instead to a state fund, so what happened was that the typical firm paid 2.7 percent to their state fund and the remaining 0.3 percent to the federal government. Then, if workers became unemployed, they could receive unemployment compensation. This unemployment compensation built an important automatic stabilizer into the economy.

The Social Security Act was apparently yet another factor hindering the economic recovery. Brown presents evidence that federal fiscal policy was more contractionary in 1937 than during any other year of the New Deal era, and imposition of the social security tax was a major reason for this fact (1956). Vedder and Gallaway estimate that by 1938 the old-age insurance added 0.85 percent to wage costs and the unemployment compensation system another 2.2 percent (1993, 141). They go on to argue that these higher wage costs made the unemployment rate 2.21 percentage points higher than it would have been if the Social Security Act had not been passed.

11.3. The Revenue Acts of 1935 and 1936

> Its effect upon the wealthy was apoplectic . . . and Huey [Long]
> was so delighted that he moved back on the New Deal reservation.
> —*Frederick Lewis Allen describing reaction to the*
> *Revenue Act of 1935 (1940, 154)*

The antibusiness and antiwealthy attitudes of the Roosevelt administration were exhibited yet again with the Revenue Act of 1935. Roosevelt sent the bill to Congress along with the statement that "Our revenue laws have operated in many ways to the unfair advantage of the few, and they have done little to prevent an unjust concentration of wealth and economic power" (Campagna 1987, 136–37). Interesting words from the man who had just signed the Social Security Act with its extremely regressive withholding tax.

The Revenue Act of 1935 raised tax rates on incomes above $50,000 with the top bracket at 75 percent on incomes over $500,000. The corporate income tax was graduated, from 12.5 percent on net income exceeding $2,000 to 15 percent on net income over $40,000. The capital stock tax was raised, as was the estate tax. The portion of estates exempted from the tax was lowered from $50,000 to $40,000, and the tax rates were raised from 2 percent on the first $10,000 to 70 percent on the taxable portion over $50 million. Gift taxes were also raised. The tax was not a big revenue raiser. Estimates suggest that it raised around $250 million per year and caused only a slight change in the concentration of wealth (Campagna 1987, 137).[5] Other than that, its economic effects are unclear. One important aspect of the bill, however, was that its target, the upper class, developed an intense dislike of Roosevelt that Allen suggests was actual hatred (1940, 184–88). Many of these people considered Roosevelt, descended from a wealthy New York family, a traitor to his class.

During 1936 Roosevelt was once again looking for additional revenue. There were two reasons for this. First, the Supreme Court ruled the processing tax portion of the Agricultural Adjustment Act unconstitutional, which took away that source of revenue. The rest of the farm program was left intact. Second, Congress voted to send out $2.2 billion in bonus checks to World War I veterans. Because of those bonus checks, Brown estimates that federal fiscal policy during 1936 was among the most expansive of the decade, only ranking behind 1931, which was the other year Congress approved bonus checks for the veterans (1956).

Roosevelt suggested going after undistributed corporate profits as a source of tax revenue. The thinking was that wealthy owners of corporations could shelter their income from taxes by holding net income as retained earnings instead of taking it as dividend income. Congress followed Roosevelt's advice; the 1936 Revenue Act taxed undistributed corporate profits with a graduated schedule ranging from 10 percent to 27 percent, depending on how large the undistributed profits were relative to adjusted net income. To appeal to business, the bill reduced some business taxes. The capital stock tax was reduced, as was the corporate income tax on incomes below $2,000.

The undistributed profits tax provided a strong incentive for firms to pay out their income as dividends. It was also a big revenue gainer for the Treasury during 1936 and 1937. Figures reported by Hubbard and Reiss state that the tax raised $145 million in 1936 and $176 million during 1937, which turns out to be about 15 percent of normal corporate income tax revenue for those years (1989, 5). Hubbard and Reiss find that for the U.S. oil industry the tax caused a significant change in firm behavior during 1936 and 1937 in that oil firms paid out much larger proportions of profits as dividends. The law had a much smaller effect in 1938 and virtually none in 1939 because firms became more and more willing to avoid the tax by increasing their costs, and thus reducing their profits, by paying higher wages, salaries, and bonuses to employees.

11.4. A Stronger Recovery

The second New Deal period of 1935–36 was associated with a much stronger economic recovery than had taken place during 1933–34. Here are the annualized quarterly growth rates of output during the second New Deal period:

1935.I	24.8 %
1935.II	1.3 %
1935.III	10.9 %
1935.IV	21.6 %
1936.I	1.9 %
1936.II	24.3 %
1936.III	11.3 %
1936.IV	13.0 %

The economy was finally rebounding strongly, and prices were rising much more slowly than during the earlier NRA period. Yet, despite this rapid growth, the unemployment rate was barely falling. The unemployment rate during 1935 averaged 20.3 percent, and despite output growth of 13.6 percent during 1936 the unemployment rate only fell to 17.0 percent. It is difficult to ascertain just how much the New Deal programs had to do with keeping the unemployment rate high, but surely they were important. A combination of fixing farm prices, promoting labor unions, and passing a series of antibusiness tax laws would certainly have a negative impact on employment. In addition, the uncertainty experienced by the business community as a result of the frequent tax law changes (1932, 1934, 1935, 1936) must have been enormous. Since firms' investment decisions very much depend on being able to plan, an increase in uncertainty tends to reduce investment expenditures. It should not be a surprise that investment as a proportion of output was at low levels during the mid-1930s. For example, during 1935 business investment was 8 percent of GDP, although a major factor in that low level was the existence of significant excess capacity. The historical average for business investment is around 14 percent.

11.5.   Excess Reserves and the Second Recession, 1937–38

The [Federal Reserve] System failed to weigh the delayed effects of the rise in reserve requirements in August 1936, employed too blunt an instrument too vigorously; this was followed by a failure to recognize promptly that the action had misfired and that a reversal of policy was called for. All those blunders were in considerable measure a consequence of the mistaken interpretation of excess reserves and their significance.
—*Milton Friedman and Anna J. Schwartz (1963, 526)*

The Great Depression lasted longer in the United States than in any of the European countries. There are two basic reasons for this: the New Deal programs hindered recovery, and the United States suffered a serious second recession during the 1930s. Some European countries did not suffer the second recession, and those that did had much weaker versions of it.

While far milder than the horrendous 1929–33 downturn, the 1937–38 recession was, nonetheless, severe. In terms of magnitude it was on the order of the 1973–75 and 1981–82 recessions that to date are the two most serious of the post–World War II era. The 1937–38 version was, like the 1929–33 version, man-made. It was clearly caused by a combination of contractionary monetary and fiscal policies. Fiscal policy was contractionary for the reasons already cited: the social security tax went into effect in 1937, and spending was much lower than in 1936 because the veterans' bonus checks were not sent out again. Because of this contractionary fiscal policy, some people have gone so far as to call the 1937–38 recession the Roosevelt Recession. Yet that description is unfair; the Federal Reserve was far more responsible for it than Franklin Roosevelt was. The cause was excess reserves.

Excess reserves are bank reserves held in excess of the amount required. During the mid-1930s the United States was experiencing a major gold inflow, and the Federal Reserve had been passively allowing it to increase the monetary base. As a result, bank reserves grew enormously over the period and by early 1937 were far in excess of the amount required. At the start of 1934, banks held $866 million of excess reserves, and by January 1936 they held $3.0 billion. By early 1936 those excess reserves represented about one-third of the entire monetary base. Banks were holding them because interest rates on government securities were so low there was no strong incentive to convert the non—interest-paying excess reserves into interest-earning bonds. In addition, the banking industry had been through the wringer earlier in the decade with all the runs and failures. There was a strong incentive for banks to hold excess reserves in case the bank panics broke out again. Finally, loan opportunities were limited; there were few households and firms with good credit histories seeking loans.

The Federal Reserve was very concerned about these excess reserves for a number of reasons. One was the fear that those reserves might be lent out and set off another wave of overspeculation in the stock market as the Federal Reserve felt had occurred during the late 1920s (Friedman and Schwartz 1963, 523). In late 1935 Federal Reserve officials began specific discussions about these excess reserves and how they could correct the perceived problem. The question was how to extract the excess reserves out of the banking system. Federal Reserve officials discussed selling securities to accomplish their goal, but that option was dismissed because of the huge volume of securities required to soak up $3.0 billion worth of excess reserves. Since the source of Federal Reserve Banks' earnings is the interest on their securities held, reducing their interest-earning assets by such a large amount would greatly reduce their earnings. Another option available was to raise the discount rate, but that too was dismissed because of the low volume of discounting at the time (Friedman and Schwartz 1963, 520). That left one option available: raise the required reserve ratio. The Federal Reserve had been given this power by the 1935 Banking Act, and this was their chance to use it. The idea was very simple: raise the required reserve ratio and the banks would simply reclassify the reserves as required instead of excess. The excess reserves would be gone and that would be the end of the problem.

Friedman and Schwartz make it clear that the Federal Reserve officials were operating in the dark (1963, 521–27). One problem was that they really did not realize what a powerful tool changing the required reserve ratio would turn out to be. They had never tried it before. They knew they were taking a risk, but they were willing to try it. A second problem was that the Federal Reserve officials had long believed that the banks did not want the excess reserves. It never occurred to them that the banks might be holding the excess reserves because they chose to.

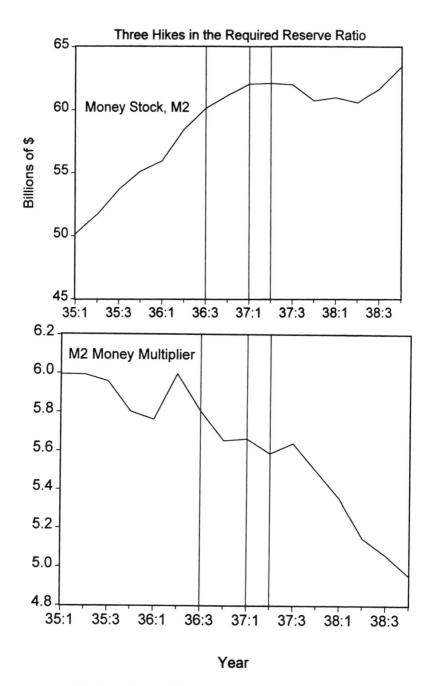

Fig. 11.1.   Effects of the hike in the required reserve ratio

The Federal Reserve went ahead and, in a series of three steps that started in August 1936 and ended in May 1937, doubled the required reserve ratio. That banks had, in fact, wanted to hold large excess reserves was evidenced when they responded by starting to rebuild their excess reserve holdings, largely by selling off some of their bank investments. Thus, the ratio of bank reserves to bank deposits began to rise, and the money multiplier fell. Meanwhile, starting in December 1936 the U.S. Treasury started to sterilize the gold flowing into the country by selling securities in the open market. Sterilization markedly slowed the growth rate of the monetary base. The net result is shown in figure 11.1. There was a sharp decline in the monetary growth rate and an actual decline in its level by mid-1937. Economists across the intellectual spectrum consider this monetary contraction to be the principal cause of the 1937–38 recession.

The recession itself was a major step backward for U.S. economic activity. It started in May 1937 and continued until June 1938. Over that period, industrial production fell about one-third, the price level fell about 3.5 percent, and at the trough the unemployment rate stood at over 19 percent. Because of this serious recession, the Great Depression was prolonged for a few more years in the United States. The misery of high unemployment and poverty continued.

CHAPTER 12

It's Finally Over

12.1. Monetary Policy

By the late summer of 1937 Federal Reserve officials realized what a serious mistake they had made in doubling the required reserve ratio. Economic output and prices were falling sharply, and the unemployment rate was rising. Meanwhile, the Roosevelt administration was catching much of the blame for the recession. Many considered the economic downturn proof that the New Deal had been an abysmal failure.[1]

In August 1937, the Federal Reserve decided they had better reverse their contractionary policies. They started a series of moves that continued through April 1938 designed to promote monetary expansion. The discount rate was lowered a half point, the required reserve ratio was reduced by a quarter, they bought $38 million of government securities, and they requested the Treasury release $300 million worth of sterilized gold (Eastburn 1965, 72). The Treasury complied with the request. These moves set off a major monetary expansion that was later augmented in September 1939 when the Federal Reserve increased their security holdings by another $380 million in response to the outbreak of war in Europe.

The results of these policies are shown in figure 12.1. The monetary expansion began in early 1938 and really gathered steam during 1939. The monetary growth rates over the period were 7.9 percent during 1939, 11.4 percent during 1940, and 12.4 percent during 1941. From 1938 to 1940 the monetary expansion was largely the result of the increasing monetary base that was caused by the Treasury's release of the gold, the Federal Reserve bond purchases, and an accelerated gold inflow during 1940. The money multiplier was falling until mid-1940 as banks continued to build up their excess reserve positions. Then, during 1940 the monetary base flattened out while the money multiplier began to rise because the reserve–deposit ratio changed course and declined sharply. The reserve–deposit ratio was falling because bank loans and investments increased significantly during 1940.

A vigorous expansion in economic output took place, but the unemployment rate remained high until 1941. Here are the rates of output growth, inflation, and unemployment during the recovery:

Year	GNP Growth	Inflation	Unemployment Rate
1938	−4.4 %	−1.3 %	19.1 %
1939	7.5 %	−1.5 %	17.2 %
1940	7.3 %	2.1 %	14.6 %
1941	15.2 %	6.3 %	9.9 %

One very encouraging feature during this period was the strength of investment spending and expenditures on consumer durables. Both of these spending components had been quite weak since 1929, and their increases during this expansion suggest that a semblance of confidence was finally returning. During the first two years of the expansion, inflation-adjusted producer durables spending rose 60 percent, residential construction increased 41 percent, and consumer durables spending went up 41 percent.

The extremely rapid output growth during 1941 was the final spurt that pushed the economy toward full employment by the end of that year.[2] Major contributors to this rise in output were expansionary U.S. fiscal policy and strong export growth.

12.2. War in Europe and the U.S. Defense Buildup

In March 1939, a Gallup poll on the question "In case war breaks out, should we sell Britain and France food supplies?" had brought a Yes from 76 percent of those [Americans] polled; in April the question was repeated and the percentage jumped from 76 to 82. In March the further question "Should we sell them airplanes and other war materials?" brought a Yes from 52 percent; in April the figure had gone way up to 66—a striking increase.

—*Frederick Lewis Allen (1940, 265)*

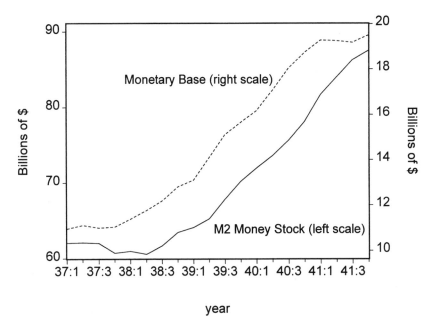

year

Fig. 12.1.   M2 money stock and monetary base, 1937–41

The major event of 1940 occurred in May when Germany invaded France. Western Europe's two major military powers were at war and, to almost everyone's shock, within just a few weeks France had surrendered and their British allies were forced into a humiliating retreat from the European continent at Dunkirk, France. These events had a significant impact on the U.S. economy for two reasons. First, Britain and her allies began placing large orders for war material from the United States and paid for it with gold. This set off a stimulus to U.S. demand from abroad, as well as the gold inflow that raised the U.S. monetary base. Second, there was great concern that the United States would be drawn into the war to support her close ally Great Britain. In preparation for that event the United States initiated a defense buildup. Federal defense expenditures, which had been $2.2 billion during 1940, rose to $13.7 billion during 1941. From 1940 to 1941 GDP rose by about $25 billion, so the increase in defense spending accounts for 46 percent of the increase in output.

Therefore, the Great Depression was ended by an enormous stimulus to aggregate demand caused by a combination of rapid monetary growth beginning in 1938 and, later, the U.S. defense buildup and increased orders for war material from Great Britain.[3] The Depression was over by late 1941 or early 1942 in the sense that the economy was close to full employment, a situation not seen since the summer of 1929.

12.3.   Cost of the Depression

The Great Depression imposed enormous costs on U.S. society. Just in terms of lost output, that is, the gap between actual output and estimated full-employment output, the Great Depression cost the United States over $2 trillion in 1972 dollars, which is roughly equivalent to three times a single year's GDP during the mid-1930s. There were numerous other costs as well, including the hardships endured by so many people in the form of hunger, social disruption, the violence associated with labor organizing, and the mental depression of the unemployed. Perhaps the greatest losses were the hundreds of thousands of young Americans who were killed or disabled while fighting in the U.S. armed forces in a war that traced its roots to economic conditions wrought by the Depression. Similar lists could be tabulated for all of the countries that experienced the Depression.

12.4.   Influence on Economic Thought

The major event that had discredited monetary policy was the juxtaposition between early 1938 and late 1940 of a weak economic recovery, explosive monetary growth, complete price rigidity, and a short term interest rate near zero. Despite a monetary growth that was rapid and constant between early 1938 and late 1941, the economy's recovery floundered until defense spending began in earnest in late 1940 . . . a chronology that ingrained a deep-seated belief in the potency of fiscal policy and the "pushing on a string" analogy for monetary policy.
                                    —*Robert J. Gordon (1980, 111)*

As Robert J. Gordon makes clear, the way the Depression ended had profound implications for macroeconomic thought. While people looking back on it years later concluded that *both* the monetary and fiscal expansions had ended the Depression, during the 1940s many reached a different conclusion. The prevailing view at the time was that the fiscal expansion had ended the Depression and that the monetary expansion had little to do with it. The fact that the fiscal stimulus appeared to return the economy to full employment was important because it confirmed the beliefs of Keynesian economists who argued that fiscal policy was more potent than monetary policy for stimulating aggregate demand. These Keynesian economists contended that monetary policy affects aggregate demand through its effect on interest rates; a monetary stimulus lowers interest rates, which causes consumption and investment spending to rise. In this way a monetary stimulus indirectly raises aggregate demand. The "pushing on a string" analogy refers to the idea that although the Federal Reserve can increase bank reserves with the intent of creating credit, this will not necessarily be effective unless the public actually walks into the banks and takes out loans. Therefore, monetary policy may be impotent, especially if interest rates are already low. If the public will not borrow at rates that are already very low, slightly lower rates will not induce much additional borrowing. A look at figure 12.2 shows that short-term interest rates were very low during the late 1930s, and the rapid monetary growth did not push them lower after 1938. The combination of rapid monetary growth, stable short-term interest rates, and the fiscal stimulus appeared to be the cause of the Depression's end. Keynesians took this to be de facto proof that their view was correct. As a result, the Keynesian view came to dominate macroeconomic thought.

Shortly after World War II ended two books were published that did much to spread the Keynesian gospel. One problem with Keynes's *General Theory of Employment, Interest, and Money* (1936) is that it is a very difficult book to read. Several sections are confusing, and terms are sometimes used interchangeably. Since not many people seemed to understand Keynes's work, it was left to those few to explain Keynes's ideas in a way accessible to others.[4] Lawrence Klein's *The Keynesian Revolution* (1947) is one such book, and it is important because it established the American version of Keynesian economics. In this book, Klein explains in great detail why he thinks fiscal policy is more potent for changing output than monetary policy, and he presents these views as though they are Keynes's ideas. The irony is that Klein misinterpreted Keynes on this point: Keynes never considered monetary policy weak; in fact he blamed the Federal Reserve and the Bank of England for causing the Depression.[5] Keynes advocated fiscal policy because he did not trust the central bankers in the United States and England! But, that aside, the important

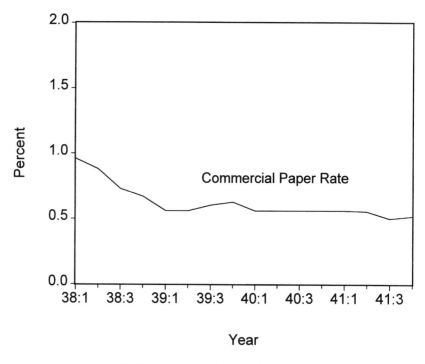

Fig. 12.2. Low short-term interest rates

point is that Klein's version of Keynes's work became "American" Keynesian economics, in which fiscal policy was considered stronger than monetary policy. The second book that was highly influential is Paul Samuelson's *Economics: An Introductory Analysis* (1948). This is the book that spread Keynesian economics to the masses because it became the preferred textbook on economic principles on college campuses around the country. The book went through numerous editions, and millions of copies were read. As a result, the Keynesian message was spread across America, and Samuelson became a very wealthy man from the book royalties.[6]

12.5. Lasting Impact of the Depression

There are several areas where the Depression had a lasting impact. First and foremost are the various government programs still in existence that were created during the 1930s. To name just a few of the more important programs, we still have social security, unemployment compensation, deposit insurance, the farm price support system, the Tennessee Valley Authority, and the Rural Electrification Administration. In fact, not only do we still have these programs, but several of them have been greatly expanded over the years. But perhaps more important than these programs are what they represent: increased involvement in the economy by the federal government. Prior to the Great Depression, the federal government was a relatively small player in the overall economy. In 1929 federal government outlays, including transfer payments and interest on the debt, were 3.8 percent of GDP. By 1939 federal outlays had risen to 6.9 percent of GDP. That trend continued, and by 1991 federal outlays were 18.6 percent of GDP.

We get a somewhat different picture if transfer payments and interest on the debt are excluded and instead we focus on government purchases of goods and services. In 1929 federal purchases were 2.2 percent of total U.S. output. In fact, during that year state and local government purchases of goods and services were almost five times larger than federal government purchases. By 1939, the last year before the big defense buildup, federal government purchases were 7.1 percent of total U.S. output, more than half as large as state and local government purchases. In 1991 federal government purchases were 7.9 percent of total U.S. output, which is about seven-tenths of state and local government purchases, similar to the situation in 1939. These figures also show that the growth of the federal government as a proportion of output since the Great Depression has been concentrated in transfer payments: collecting increasing proportions of households' total income and then turning around and passing it back in the form of social security, medicare, and all the other innumerable transfer payment programs the federal government operates.

This increased government involvement in the economy represents something else, too: the view that it is the federal government's responsibility to take care of people. Prior to the Great Depression, indigent people were taken care of by private charities and poorhouses operated by local governments. The magnitude of the poverty problem during the early 1930s simply swamped these local charitable organizations. They did not have the resources to begin to deal with all of the cases, so the federal government stepped in to fill the gap. Over time the federal government took control of dealing with the impoverished away from state and local governments and stayed in control for the next 60 years.

Another area where the Great Depression had a lasting impact is on American politics. The Democratic party gained control of Congress in the 1932 election and for the most part had pretty much continuous control for the next 60 years, especially in the House of Representatives. It remains to be seen whether the 1994 and 1996 congressional election results represent a genuine break of that record of Democratic control.

Finally, the Great Depression has obviously had a lasting impact on economics for the simple reason that the branch called macroeconomics was developed during the 1930s. The Great Depression was the impetus for Keynes to write his *General Theory*, which marks the development of modern macroeconomics.

In conclusion, the Great Depression was the seminal macroeconomic event of the twentieth century. It is important not just because it caused such a prolonged period of high unemployment, but also because it caused so many other major changes to occur. Arguably, the most important changes occurred in Germany and the United States, which, not surprisingly, were the two major countries that suffered the worst output declines. Germany ended up with Adolf Hitler who spread his poison throughout Europe. The United States ended up with Franklin Roosevelt who was the principal agent in setting up the U.S. welfare state.

CHAPTER 13

A Summing Up; and
Could It Happen Again?

⎯⎯▷•◁⎯⎯

Those who cannot remember the past are condemned to repeat
it.

—*George Santayana*

What has happened once will invariably happen again when the
same set of circumstances which combined to produce it shall
combine in the same way.

—*Abraham Lincoln*

⎯⎯▷•◁⎯⎯

13.1. Answers to Questions Posed Earlier

In chapter 1 several questions were listed that we have attempted to
answer in this book. Here are short summary answers to those questions.

*Did factors building up during the 1920s set the stage for the Great
Depression?*

The answer would appear to be yes, but they were not nearly as
important as the mistakes policymakers made during the late 1920s and
early 1930s. There is enough evidence to suggest that residential construction was overbuilt by the late 1920s, enough so that it was declining
on its own and probably would have declined further even without the
appearance of the serious Depression. Also, the stock market may have
been a speculative bubble, although the evidence on this point is mixed.

The arguments about the worsening income distribution during the 1920s have some merit because the data confirm that there was, in fact, a worsening distribution during that period. Yet that factor hardly seems likely to have caused the Great Depression.

Why was the 1929–33 recession so severe?

The short answer here is bank failures. Policymakers made several mistakes, but none worse than the Federal Reserve's inactivity during the widespread bank failures during 1931 and then again during the last wave that started in late 1932 and ended in March 1933. Thousands of banks suspended payments or went bankrupt. The widespread fear of more failures caused the public to hoard currency. The money stock and spending plummeted as a result.

Why did the Depression last so long?

There appear to be three reasons for this. First is the severity of the 1929–33 recession. The decline in output was so large that it was probably going to take a few years to get back to full employment anyway since major changes in economic activity take time to occur. The evidence from Germany supports this point: they had a massive public works program and a huge monetary expansion, and it still took that country about four years to get out of the Depression, simply because they were starting from such a low point in 1932.

Second was the New Deal. Many of its programs were poorly thought out and did little to stimulate output. In fact, as we argued in chapters 9 and 11, several of the programs were both contractionary and inflationary.

The third reason is that the United States had a serious recession during 1937 and 1938. Output was already well below full employment when the recession began, and when the downturn was over, the economy had moved even further away from full employment. Despite very rapid monetary growth and a big fiscal expansion later, it took more than three years after the recession ended to get the economy back up to full employment.

Why was it worldwide?

The Great Depression was a worldwide event because countries were on the gold standard and had fixed exchange rates. The sequence of events described in chapters 4, 5, and 6 shows how it happened: Britain went back onto the gold standard in 1925 at the wrong exchange rate, and the United States did not play by the gold standard rules until they underwent the monetary expansion in 1927. That monetary policy was reversed in 1928 to stop the stock market advance. The resulting high U.S. short-term interest rates resulting from the monetary contraction caused gold to flow from other countries into the United States. Those countries responded by raising their own interest rates to protect their gold stocks, and by doing so they started recessions in their own countries.

Why was the U.S. economy unable to grow during the mid-1930s without a significant acceleration of inflation?

It does seem amazing that the inflation rate accelerated significantly during the mid-1930s while the unemployment rate was 22 percent in 1934, 20 percent in 1935, and 17 percent in 1936. How could the price level rise at an increasing rate with so much excess capacity in the economy? The most plausible answer seems to be that the New Deal programs, with their emphasis on raising prices and wages, were the cause. This is the conclusion economists have reached on this question.

Why did the reserve–deposit and currency–deposit ratios rise so dramatically during the 1930s?

Once again, the answer is bank failures. The public became increasingly fearful of bank failures during the first few years of the 1930s, and rightly so. Their motive was to convert bank deposits into currency, thus the currency–deposit ratio rose. Meanwhile, bank managers were worried that bank runs might develop, so their incentive was to increase their excess reserve positions, which drove up the reserve–deposit ratio. The net result was a plunging money multiplier that dragged the money stock down with it.

What is interesting is that once President Roosevelt declared the National Bank Holiday in March 1933, then established deposit insurance in 1934, the public became confident in the banking system and started redepositing currency into banks. Bank managers, however, continued to build up their excess reserve positions until 1940, although it is not clear how much of that increase was due to fear of bank runs and how much was due to the very low short-term interest rates prevailing at the time.

What caused the Depression to end?

A combination of very rapid monetary growth that began in 1938, the 1940 increase in sales of war material to Britain, and the U.S. defense buildup that also began in 1940.

13.2.   Could It Happen Again?

The standard answer is no, that what converted a garden variety recession into the Great Depression was a disastrous series of policy errors. Neither the Federal Reserve Board nor the Congress would be so silly now as to repeat those mistakes. The Fed would not allow the banking system to collapse. It would not permit the money supply to decline by a third. Congress would not raise taxes in a slump. Hence there is no reason to fear another Great Depression.

—Barry Eichengreen, who thinks it could *happen*
again (1992a, 2)

My teachers regarded the depression as largely the product of misguided governmental policy—or at least as greatly intensified by such policies. They blamed the monetary and fiscal authorities for permitting banks to fail and quantity of deposits to decline. Far from preaching the need to let deflation and bankruptcy run their course, they issued repeated pronunciamentos calling for governmental action to stem the deflation.

—Milton Friedman, who was a graduate student at the
University of Chicago during the Great Depression
(1970, 163)

Could it happen again? Sure it could; there is no reason why policymakers could not make a set of mistakes similar to those made in the late 1920s and early 1930s and set off another Great Depression. While it is true that those mistakes made years ago were made from economic ignorance, it is also clear that anyone in authority trying to end the Depression could have contacted Milton Friedman's economics instructors at the University of Chicago and asked for ideas. In other words, during the 1930s the economic knowledge existed to end the Depression, but the political leaders in power were not listening to the economists with productive ideas.

This exact same thing goes on today. As a group, economists in the United States are not really listened to. To cite just a few examples, if economists' advice was followed, we would probably not have a minimum wage law, our laws against illegal narcotics would probably be very different, the resources devoted to primary and secondary education would be much greater than they currently are, and the federal tax code would be drastically different from the one now in place. So it would certainly be possible for a group of leaders in control of our government and the Federal Reserve to appear on the scene and pursue a series of disastrous policies that destroy the economy, all the while ignoring what economists have to say about it. It has happened before, and it could happen again.

At the same time, there are reasons to be optimistic. One reason is the existence of deposit insurance. With federally insured bank deposits, it is highly unlikely that we would ever experience the widespread bank panics like those that occurred during the early 1930s.

Another reason to be optimistic is because of the existence of automatic stabilizers built into our fiscal system that either did not exist in the early 1930s or were much less important than they currently are. Unemployment compensation and the various federal welfare systems in place for the impoverished provide a safety net to help support aggregate demand during periods of falling output. Another important automatic stabilizer is the federal income tax. Since tax rates are much higher today than during the early 1930s, the graduated income tax plays a much greater stabilizer role than it did during the 1930s. Many economists feel that the combination of these automatic stabilizers and deposit insurance provides our greatest defense against another Great Depression.

Finally, macroeconomists have been able to make some inroads into educating policymakers. For example, during the severe 1981–82 recession no one advocated raising tax rates to balance the budget (as was done in 1932). Instead, they passed the Economic Recovery Tax Act of 1981, which reduced tax rates. Another example was the Federal Reserve's reaction to the 1987 stock market crash. The day it occurred the Chairman of the Federal Reserve Board of Governors, Alan Greenspan, appeared before television cameras and announced that the nation's central bank stood ready to provide liquidity to the financial system. During the weeks immediately following the crash the Federal Reserve flooded the financial system with liquidity to prevent the crash from spreading. A few weeks later they quietly removed the excess liquidity from the system. They were highly praised for their efforts, and Milton Friedman gave them his highest compliment: he said they had done exactly what he would have done![1]

So there are several good reasons to think that it will not happen again. Yet at the same time it is important to realize that it could happen again if a perverse set of policies were carried out by well-meaning, ignorant people as was the case during the late 1920s and early 1930s. After all, never say never.

Notes

Chapter 1

1. The Depression was also a factor in the rise of the militarists in Japan, although apparently not the major one. See Sadler 1946, 264–66.

2. For a discussion of Keynes's contributions to the development of modern macroeconomics, see Hall 1990, 47–54.

3. To put that unemployment rate in perspective, the highest unemployment rate the U.S. has experienced since World War II occurred in November 1982 when the rate hit 10.6 percent.

4. Fisher's equation of interest rates is $r = i + p^e$ where r is the nominal interest rate, i is the real interest rate, and p^e is the expected inflation rate. The real rate is ex ante because it is a forward-looking view of what we expect the inflation rate to be over some future period. An ex post real interest rate is computed as $i = r - p$ where p is the actual inflation rate that occurred. Here, we are taking a backward-looking view of what actually happened.

5. The money multiplier is inversely related to cd. This is because if, for a given monetary base, we decided to hold more currency and fewer bank deposits, funds would flow out of the banking system as we converted deposits into currency. This outflow of funds from the system means that fewer bank reserves exist to support deposits. Therefore, other things being equal, a rise in cd reduces the stock of money. The money multiplier is also inversely related to the reserve–deposit ratio (rd).

Chapter 2

1. The idea that production experience results in productivity gains is called learning by doing. Lucas (1993) discusses this concept as a source of economic growth and presents some evidence.

2. Net household formation is equal to the change in occupied dwelling units.

3. Construction of the Empire State Building began in the late 1920s. It was not completed until 1931.

4. This is a standard result in consumption theory and has strong empirical support from cross-sectional data.

5. For a discussion of the underconsumptionist school of thought, see Haberler 1958. This argument has also been applied to the 1980s and 1990s.

6. A margin account allows an individual to purchase stock where the individual puts up some of the funds and borrows the rest (the margin) from the broker.

7. Actually, ignoring taxes and sales commissions, a shareholder would have had to experience a gain in stock prices of 5.64 percent over a year, the differential between the call rate and the dividend yield, to break even. Given the gains in stock prices from 1927 to September 1929, such an expected gain was certainly reasonable.

8. Rappaport and White's results are challenged by Liu, Santoni, and Stone (1995) who argue that the increased interest-rate spread was due to restrictive monetary policy, not speculative excess.

9. Var(u) is unobservable, thus it drops out in the empirical test.

10. Curtis-Wright was the only unprofitable firm whose stock price was used to compute the DJIA in 1929. Sirkin excluded it from the sample.

11. A study by Diba and Grossman (1988) uses more sophisticated statistical tests than Santoni uses and reaches the same conclusion.

Chapter 3

1. A grain is a measure of weight equivalent to 0.002083 ounces.

2. The motivation for Britain's return to the gold standard is discussed in chapter 4.

Chapter 4

1. The casualty figures cited in this chapter are taken from *Information Please Almanac 1995*.

2. The output and price data are from Aldcroft 1970, 32. The unemployment data are from Garside 1990, 4.

3. The greatest critic of the return to gold was Keynes, and he was quite strident in his attack. For the best example, see Keynes 1925.

4. See Pope and Hoyle 1985, 104–8, for a discussion of coal production by Britain and its European competitors.

5. The United States sterilized the gold flow to prevent inflation. This is discussed in more detail in chapter 6. France sold foreign currencies for gold and then simply held the gold. They apparently did not understand that they were breaking the rules of the gold standard. See Moure 1991, chap. 2.

6. Benjamin Strong was an interesting character who had a major impact on U.S. economic events during the 1920s. For a discussion of Strong and his importance, see Chandler 1958.

7. See, for example, Friedman and Schwartz 1963 or Kindleberger 1986.

8. The recession Britain experienced was mild compared to the recessions in most other countries. Most economists believe that Britain did not have a severe

recession because they never experienced a big boom during the 1920s. See, for example, Aldcroft 1983, 16.

9. Because of various contingencies in the agreement, it is impossible to determine how many years Germany would have had to make payments on these reparations. What was clear, however, was that "Germany would be obligated to make substantial transfers over a period of decades" (Eichengreen 1992b, 131).

10. To get a sense of how large these German budget deficits were, consider that the U.S. budget deficits of the 1980s that had so many people concerned peaked in 1983 at 6.3 percent of GDP (Council of Economic Advisors 1993).

11. The 1923 explosion in money creation was also partly the result of the German response to the French and Belgians occupying the Ruhr region in retaliation for not receiving the reparations fast enough. The German government responded by urging the citizens of the region to resist passively, and, to help them accomplish this, the government printed money to subsidize both the citizens and industry.

12. The level of velocity depends on the price level, while the rate of change in velocity depends on the inflation rate.

13. The growth rates in table 4.2 are approximations because the monetary growth rate is proxied by currency growth.

14. *Rediscounting* is the process by which a central bank, in this case the Reichsbank, provides liquidity to banks. The central bank creates bank reserves that are lent to banks. The rate charged is called the *rediscount rate*. The banks that are borrowing from the central bank must put up collateral such as bonds or commercial paper. When the Reichsbank announced that they would no longer rediscount government bonds, they were effectively saying that they would no longer monetize the government budget deficits.

15. Charles Dawes won the 1925 Nobel Peace Prize for his efforts.

16. Eichengreen (1992b, 244–45) argues that fiscal policy was contractionary as well.

17. There is some disagreement about whether the tax increases were more important for stabilizing the franc or whether Poincaré's ability to reestablish confidence was the key factor. See Eichengreen 1992b, 182–83.

Chapter 5

1. The yield curve often inverts prior to economic recessions. For a discussion, see Hall 1990, 214.

2. The stock index figures cited here are taken from Galbraith 1954.

3. This explanation is consistent with the q theory of investment originally suggested by Keynes (1936) and formalized by Tobin and Brainard (1968).

4. The effect of uncertainty in the money demand function is formalized by Mascaro and Meltzer (1983). For a discussion of why uncertainty would have a greater impact on spending on durables than on nondurables and services, see Romer 1990. Flacco and Parker (1992) provide empirical support for the proposition that the increased uncertainty reduced consumption expenditures.

5. Temin (1976) suggests that Friedman and Schwartz contend that only monetary factors were responsible for the output decline of 1930. He misinter-

prets them on this point; Friedman and Schwartz (1963, 306–7) make it clear that both monetary contraction and the increased demand for money generated the contraction during 1930.

6. Burbidge and Harrison (1985) reach a similar conclusion about the period 1929–31 from estimates generated from a vector autoregression model.

7. The data are from the *National Income and Product Accounts, 1929–1974* (Washington, D.C.: U.S. Government Printing Office, 1976).

8. See Alston 1983 for a detailed discussion about the farmers' debt problems during the 1920s and 1930s. Farm prices fell faster than the general price level because there was a bumper crop in 1928 that was being held in storage. As the Depression worsened, financing to hold the inventories became increasingly difficult to obtain, so the inventories were sold and prices plummeted. See Kindleberger 1986, 73–74.

9. A number of studies have addressed the issue of whether the deflation of the early 1930s was expected or not. This is an important issue because if it had been expected, then ex ante real interest rates would have been incredibly high because in Fisher's equation of interest rates $r = i - p^e$ expected deflation implies that the last term is negative and since it is being subtracted it takes on a positive value. A high ex ante real rate would suggest that some major shock to the productivity of capital occurred. However, these studies tend to confirm the opposite, that the deflation was unexpected. Therefore, ex ante real interest rates were not unusually high, although ex post real rates were quite high. For a discussion, see Hamilton 1992 and Evans and Wachtel 1993.

10. Since the Depression appears to have been unexpected, the expectations effect was probably small. DeLong and Summers (1986) report correlations between prices and output that suggest that falling prices are consistent with falling output. However, their channel is different from that being described here; they contend that falling prices raised real interest rates, which reduced investment expenditures.

Chapter 6

1. This statistic and the remaining money and banking statistics in this chapter are taken from Board of Governors of the Federal Reserve System 1943.

2. Britain's decision to leave the gold standard is discussed in more detail in chapter 7.

Chapter 7

1. The U.S. price level data are taken from Gordon 1993. Unless otherwise indicated, the data referred to in this section are taken from the League of Nations *Monthly Bulletin of Statistics* (Geneva, various issues).

2. See Kindleberger 1986, 154–58, for a detailed discussion of Britain's political problems during the summer of 1931.

3. The Bank of England was apparently a little slow reacting to the crisis, and one of the reasons cited was that Montague Norman, the head of the Bank, was ill. See Eichengreen 1992, 281.

4. Twenty-five other countries followed Britain off gold. These countries were mostly those of the British empire as well as Britain's major trading partners that were not part of the empire. See Kindleberger 1986, 159.

5. The Bank of England's bank rate is the equivalent of the discount rate in the United States; that is, it is the rate on a loan from the Bank of England to a bank.

6. The rapid rise in unemployment was also apparently due to the unusual rigidity of nominal wages. See O'Brien 1985.

7. Gold flowed from Germany to France, but the French were sterilizing it. Canada had no bank failures, yet had a Depression as severe as the United States experienced. See Haubrich 1990 for a discussion of the Canadian experience.

8. Economically, the Soviet Union was almost totally isolated from the rest of the world at this time, and its economic statistics were probably completely untrustworthy anyway. See Bernanke 1995 for a discussion of the role of wage flexibility in explaining the magnitude of output declines across countries.

Chapter 8

1. See Campagna 1987, 98–99, for the details of the Revenue Act of 1932.

2. Hoover also tried some other approaches to stimulate the economy, none of which were especially successful. See Campagna 1987, 90–100, for details.

3. This is the so-called scissors effect in action whereby a major change in open market operations is partially offset by an opposite reaction in the quantity of discounting.

4. See Friedman and Schwartz 1963, 386–89, for a detailed discussion of the dissension within the Federal Reserve and the reasons for halting the program. Also see Epstein and Ferguson 1984 for further discussion.

5. Bernanke (1983) presents a case that the Depression turned into a Great Depression because the bank failures broke the financial intermediation function of banks and created a massive credit crunch. See Meltzer 1995 for criticism of Bernanke's thesis.

6. Bernanke and Parkinson 1991 argue that the U.S. experience during the 1930s is not consistent with a real business cycle model because the 1930s were not characterized by productivity shocks.

7. McCallum (1990) presents results that suggest that if the Federal Reserve had followed a policy of targeting the growth of the monetary base, the Great Depression would have been a relatively minor recession. Fackler and Randall (1994) reach a similar conclusion.

Chapter 9

1. Hitler became chancellor in January 1933, but did not obtain his dictatorial powers until March 1933 when the German Parliament passed the Law for Alleviating the Distress of People and Reich (better known as the Enabling Act) in the hysteria following the burning of Reichstag (the German Parliamentary building) by a communist. For a discussion of Hitler's rise to power, see Toland 1976, especially chapter 11.

2. The abrogation of gold clauses was challenged in court, but in 1935 the Supreme Court, in a 5–4 decision, backed the Roosevelt administration. See Degen 1987, 79.

3. See Flood 1992 for a survey of the debate over deposit insurance that took place during the early 1930s.

4. A recent study by Kroszner and Rajan (1994) finds no evidence that banks were taking on excessive risk by underwriting securities.

5. The Federal Open Market Committee replaced the Open Market Policy Committee that had been set up in 1923.

6. Another important change imposed on the financial industry was the creation of the Securities and Exchange Commission (SEC). Through the Securities Act of 1933 and the Securities Exchange Act of 1934, the SEC was created and empowered to ensure that new stock offerings were registered and that the public was supplied with accurate information about the companies issuing equity. In addition, the Federal Reserve Board was given the authority to set margin requirements. See Chandler 1970, 157–58, for more detail.

7. Friedman and Schwartz (1963) report the deposit–currency ratio. Here, we are discussing the currency–deposit ratio, which is just the inverse of Friedman and Schwartz's data series.

8. A yield of .0005 implies that a three-month Treasury bill with a face value of $10,000 would cost $9,998.75. In other words, the purchaser would earn $1.25 in interest income over the three month holding period.

9. There are always proposals to alter or abolish the Federal Reserve but they are usually ignored. However, when the Federal Reserve is blamed for causing economic distress, some people in Congress start to pay attention to anti–Federal Reserve legislation. Such was the case during and shortly after the 1981–82 recession.

10. These are just the general conditions set forth by the NRA. There were numerable exception clauses not discussed here. See Chandler 1970 for more detail.

11. A company union was a labor union controlled by the firm that employed the unionized workers.

12. Cooper and Haltiwanger (1993) show that one area where the NRA did have positive aspects was in stabilizing employment over the course of a year in the automotive industry that previously had been subject to wide seasonal fluctuations.

13. This discussion of the AAA is relatively brief and ignores several facets of the complicated program. Readers seeking more detail should see Chandler 1970, 215–19.

14. Weinstein (1980), in an exhaustive study of the NIRA, provides estimates that suggest that during the time when the NRA was in force it was responsible for about a 14 percent annual rate of increase in prices and a 26 percent annual increase in wages. Vedder and Gallaway 1993, 137–42, also conclude that the NIRA greatly hindered the recovery.

15. See Reading 1973 and Wright 1974 for New Deal expenditures by state and an analysis of the factors determining those expenditures.

Chapter 10

1. Our primary interest here is in the area of economics, so we do not discuss the Nazis' treatment of their political opposition once they were in power. Interested readers can consult a wide number of sources. See, for example, Shirer 1960 or Toland 1976.

2. See, for example, Sohn-Rethel 1978.

3. While there were several different versions of such bills, Work Creation Bills were the most important for raising funds.

4. Overy (1982, 60) disputes this conclusion and contends that the actual number was much smaller.

5. The estimates of real wage changes over the period vary dramatically. For example, over the period 1933–1937 Bonnell (1981) shows that real wages fell 11 percent, Nathan (1944, 185) reports that they fell about 5 percent, while Temin (1989, 121) cites figures showing that they rose 11 percent. Given the behavior of consumption expenditures described in the text, it seems likely that the lower estimates are closer to the truth.

6. See Nathan 1944, chapter 4, for a detailed discussion of the Food Estate.

7. This is what Hitler had to say about prices: "Inflation does not arise when money enters circulation, but only when the individual demands more money for the same service. Here we must intervene. That is what I had to explain to [Economics Minister] Schacht, that the first cause of the stability of our currency is the concentration camp" (taken from James, 1986, 353).

8. Many of the inmates at the notorious Auschwitz concentration camp worked at a nearby synthetic oil plant.

9. Germany attacked western Europe first because the leading Army officers convinced Hitler that they had to neutralize their western flank before focusing on the east.

Chapter 11

1. The Banking Act of 1935, which reorganized the Federal Reserve and explicitly told the Fed to accept government securities as eligible paper, was discussed in chapter 9.

2. Another prolabor bill passed during this period was the Fair Labor Standards Act of 1938. This law specified a national minimum wage of 25 cents per hour and required employers to pay a 50 percent premium for work in excess of forty hours per week.

3. O'Brien (1985) reports wage hikes one year prior to every U.S. recession from 1892–1975 and finds that the wage hikes during 1936–37 were the third highest in his sample.

4. Bernanke and Parkinson (1989) consider the real wage behavior during the 1930s from an efficiency wage point of view.

5. Tax hikes aimed at the upper income groups often do not yield high revenues because the wealthy are well positioned to take advantage of loopholes in the law.

Chapter 12

1. Due in part to public dissatisfaction over the New Deal, Republicans scored major gains in the 1938 congressional elections.

2. The 9.9 percent unemployment rate during 1941 is somewhat misleading since it is an annual average. The unemployment rate during the fourth quarter was 7.4 percent. The rate was down to 5.0 percent by the second quarter of 1942.

3. There is some disagreement over the relative contributions of each. For example, Degen (1987, 101–3) and Friedman and Schwartz (1963, 550) argue that both monetary and fiscal expansions were important, while Romer (1992) contends that monetary policy was far more important than fiscal policy. Burbidge and Harrison (1985) also find strong evidence for money's role during the period from 1938 to 1941.

4. Keynes was not around to explain his ideas because he died in 1946.

5. This difference between Keynes's economics and Keynesian economics was not pointed out until Leijunhufvud's (1968) work was published.

6. Both Klein and Samuelson went on to win Nobel Prizes in economics, although not for these books. Klein was awarded the prize for his work in econometrics and forecasting, Samuelson for his work in incorporating mathematics into economic theory.

Chapter 13

1. Remember, however, that the Federal Reserve Bank of New York followed a similar policy in late 1929.

Glossary

Arbitrage - the process of buying in one market and then selling in another for a profit. This process kept the foreign exchange rate constant under the gold standard because if the exchange rate made the price of gold in one country different from the price in another country, then an arbitrage possibility existed and profiteers would ship gold from the country where it was less valuable to the country where it was more valuable. In doing so the exchange rate would get bid back to where the price of gold was the same in both countries.

Bagehot, Walter (1826–77) - editor of the London *Economist* from 1861–77. In 1873 his book *Lombard Street* was published. It went on to become known as the "bible" for central bankers.

Bank Rate - the term used in Britain and in Europe for the rate on a loan from the central bank to a bank. It is equivalent to the discount rate in the United States.

Bill of Acceptance (Banker's acceptance) - this is a security issued by a bank, which directs the bank to pay a stated party a specific amount of money at a given future date. It represents a method of short-term borrowing by banks. When the Federal Reserve sells or buys securities in the open market to change bank reserves, it deals in U.S. Treasury bills, notes, and bonds, and also banker's acceptances.

Clearinghouses - a consortium of banks would gather at a clearinghouse to clear checks and lend each other reserves. The clearinghouses offered banks protection in the event of bank runs; a solvent bank experiencing a run could borrow reserves from other members of the clearinghouse until sanity was restored. Once the Federal Reserve was established, the clearinghouse system was no longer deemed necessary.

Commercial Paper - low-risk short-term debt issued by nonfinancial corporations, typically to fund inventory holdings. Under the real bills doctrine, commercial paper was the predominant financial instrument accepted by the Federal Reserve as collateral for discount loans to member banks.

Currency–Deposit Ratio - the ratio of currency in the hands of the public to bank deposits. Bank runs caused the currency–deposit ratio to rise.

Discount Rate - rate charged on a discount loan from the Federal Reserve to a bank. This rate is an administered rate in that it is set by the Federal Reserve.

Discounting - loans from Federal Reserve banks to member banks. These loans are newly created base money because the Federal Reserve simply credits the borrowing bank's balances at the Federal Reserve or issues the loan in the form of currency.

Eligible Paper - the term used by the Federal Reserve to describe what they would accept as collateral for loans (discounts) to member banks. Under the real bills doctrine, only commercial paper and bankers' acceptances were eligible paper.

External Drain - occurs when people remove financial capital from a country. For example, an external drain from the United States would occur if investors suddenly lost confidence in the U.S. economy or there were fears of a dollar depreciation. In response, they would sell their dollar-denominated financial assets like U.S. stocks and bonds and move their financial capital to another country. Under the gold standard, the external drain took the form of a gold outflow.

Fisher, Irving (1867–1947) - Famous American economist who worked at Yale. He is best known for presenting the equation of exchange, which describes nominal GDP as equaling the product of the money stock and velocity, and his equation of interest rates, which is the relationship between nominal interest rates, real interest rates, and expected inflation. In 1929 Fisher proclaimed that stock prices would stay high. He lost his shirt in the ensuing crash.

Friedman, Milton (1912–) - Nobel Prize–winning American economist who taught for years at the University of Chicago and now works at the Hoover Institution. He is the dominant monetarist economist in the world and, along with Anna Schwartz, wrote the *Monetary History of the United States, 1867–1960*, which is considered both the empirical foundation of monetarism and one of the greatest books ever written in macroeconomics.

Galbraith, John Kenneth (1908–) - American economist who taught at Harvard for many years. He is the author of several books covering a wide range of topics, including *The Great Crash* in which he argues that the stock market advance of the late 1920s was a speculative bubble.

GDP - see Gross Domestic Product.

GDP Deflator - a price index that measures the average prices of final goods and services produced within an economy. The GDP deflator equals 100 in the base year. Year-to-year percent changes in the GDP deflator provide an estimate of the inflation rate.

Gold Flow - gold movements from one country to another. When gold flowed into a country it would be deposited in banks and thus become bank reserves and base money. A gold outflow reduced bank reserves and the monetary base. See also *Sterilization*.

Gold Standard - the system whereby a government would fix the price of gold and then have money made out of gold and/or paper money backed by gold.

Under this system, as long as gold flows were not sterilized, changes in a country's stock of money were greatly influenced by gold inflows and outflows. If gold flowed into a county, the stock of money rose; if gold flowed out, the stock of money fell. Also, if two countries were on the gold standard, then the exchange rate between their two currencies would be fixed. See also *Rules of the Game*.

Government Securities - bonds, notes, and bills issued by a government's treasury to fund budget deficits.

Gross Domestic Product (GDP) - the value of all of the final goods and services produced within the boundaries of a country during a year. GDP differs from GNP (gross national product) in that GDP is production within a country while GNP is production by that country's citizens. In other words, for the United States GDP is the dollar value of output produced within the fifty states regardless of who produced it. GNP does not measure output produced by foreigners living in the United States, but does measure output produced by U.S. citizens living outside the United States. The nominal value is just the output valued at current prices while the real value is output measured at a base year's prices to allow comparisons over time adjusted for inflation.

Harrison, George L. (1887–1958) - became Governor of the Federal Reserve Bank of New York following Benjamin Strong's death in 1928 and headed that bank until 1941. A lawyer by training, he nevertheless had a solid understanding of monetary affairs. He was responsible for the open market purchases following the stock market crash in October 1929 that Friedman and Schwartz consider responsible for keeping the crash from spreading to the banking sector and for the 1932 open market purchase program. During the early 1930s he was all too often the lone voice of sanity among the top Federal Reserve officials. Unfortunately, for the most part no one was listening.

Hoover, Herbert (1874–1964) - a mining engineer with a worldwide reputation, he headed several international food relief efforts both in Asia and Europe before serving as Commerce Secretary. He was elected president in 1928 and took office in 1929. He was voted out of office in the 1932 election because of public dissatisfaction over the extremely poor economic conditions.

Internal Drain - occurs when the public loses confidence in the banking system and converts their bank deposits into currency.

Keynes, John Maynard (1883–1946) - the great British economist who wrote *The General Theory of Employment, Interest, and Money*, which develops the framework of modern macroeconomics. He held a variety of posts with the British government and taught at Cambridge University for several years. He was part of the British delegation to the Paris Peace Conference following World War I, and he headed the British delegation to the Bretton Woods conference in 1944.

Kindleberger, Charles P. (1910–) - American economist who taught at MIT for many years. He has written several books, one of which is *The World in Depression* where he argues that worldwide deflation was a major factor that turned the recessions experienced by many countries into depressions.

Monetary Base - the amount of currency in the hands of the public plus bank reserves. The central bank controls the monetary base by issuing discounts (which increase the base) and buying and selling government securities. For example, when the Federal Reserve buys securities they print the funds to do so, and when the funds are deposited into banks the base rises. When the Federal Reserve sells bonds, the monetary base falls. The monetary base multiplied by the money multiplier equals the stock of money, or $M = (1 + cd)/(cd + rd)B$, where M is the stock of money, cd is the currency–deposit ratio, rd is the reserve–deposit ratio, and B is the monetary base.

Money Multiplier - the amount by which a \$1 increase in the monetary base causes the stock of money to rise. The formula for the money multiplier is $(1 + cd)/(cd + rd)$ where cd is the currency–deposit ratio and rd is the reserve–deposit ratio. The money multiplier is inversely related to both cd and rd.

Parity Ratio - under the gold standard the parity ratio was the government-set price of gold in one country relative to the government-set price of gold in another country. The parity ratio implied a fixed rate of exchange between the two countries' currencies. For example, if the United States set the price of gold at \$20 U.S. per ounce, and Canada set the price at \$20 Canadian per ounce, then the exchange rate between the U.S. dollar and the Canadian dollar would be 1:1 to make the value of an ounce of gold the same in both countries.

Real Bills Doctrine - the idea that credit creation should be used to support "real economic activity," which in this view was only represented by commercial paper. Firms issue commercial paper to fund the production of goods and services. Operationally, this meant that the Federal Reserve only accepted commercial paper (real bills) as collateral for discounts (credit creation).

Reserve–Deposit Ratio - the ratio of bank reserves (both required and excess) to bank deposits. When bank runs occurred, managers of banks not experiencing runs would increase their reserve–deposit ratio to help protect their bank if a run started on it.

Roosevelt, Franklin D. (1882–1945) - served as Secretary of the Navy and governor of New York before becoming president in 1933. He held that office until his death in 1945. He was the principal architect of the New Deal.

Rules of the Game - Under the rules of the gold standard governments had to do the following: (1) maintain a fixed gold price, (2) buy and sell as much gold as the public supplies and demands, (3) allow the free flow of gold across borders, and (4) not sterilize gold inflows and outflows.

Samuelson, Paul (1915–) - Nobel Prize winning American economist who spent his career at MIT. He is credited with incorporating mathematics into economic theory and in this way has had an enormous impact on the economics profession. An adherent to the Keynesian view, he is one of the best known economists in the world, in large part because his textbook *Economics: An Introductory Analysis* was widely used in college level principles classes for decades.

Schwartz, Anna J. (1915–) - One of the world's leading monetarist economists, she has worked for many years at the National Bureau of Economic

Research in New York. She coauthored the *Monetary History of the United States, 1867–1960* with Milton Friedman. This book is considered both the empirical foundation of monetarism and one of the greatest books ever written in macroeconomics.

Sterilization - the process by which a central bank prevents a gold flow from causing the monetary base to change. If, for example, $1 million worth of gold flowed into the United States and the Federal Reserve did nothing, the monetary base would rise by $1 million. If, however, the Federal Reserve wanted to prevent the base from rising, they would sterilize the $1 million gold inflow by simply selling $1 million worth of government securities.

Strong, Benjamin (1872–1928) - Governor of the Federal Reserve Bank of New York from 1914 until his death in 1928. He is credited with establishing the Federal Reserve Open Market Policy Committee in 1923, which, under his control, determined Federal Reserve policy during the 1920s.

Bibliography

Aldcroft, Derek H. 1970. *The Interwar Economy: Britain, 1919–1939*. London: B. T. Batsford.

———. 1983. *The British Economy Between the Wars*. Oxford: Philip Allan Publishers.

Allen, Frederick Lewis. 1931. *Only Yesterday*. New York: Harper and Brothers.

———. 1940. *Since Yesterday*. New York: Harper and Row.

Alston, Lee J. 1983. "Farm Foreclosures in the United States During the Interwar Period." *Journal of Economic History* 43 (December): 885–903.

Angell, Wayne. 1989. "Monetary Policy in a Centrally Planned Economy: Restructuring Toward a Market-Oriented Socialist System." Paper presented at the Institute of the USA and Canada, Moscow, September 4.

Armstrong, Louise V. 1938. *We Too Are the People*. Boston: Little, Brown, and Co.

Bagehot, Walter. 1873. *Lombard Street*. Reprinted in *The Collected Works of Walter Bagehot*. London: The Economist, 1978.

Balke, Nathan S., and Robert J. Gordon. 1986. "Appendix B: Historical Data." In Robert J. Gordon, ed., *The American Business Cycle: Continuity and Change*. Chicago: University of Chicago Press.

Bellush, Bernard. 1975. *The Failure of the NRA*. New York: W. W. Norton.

Bernanke, Ben S. 1983. "Nonmonetary Effects of the Financial Crisis in the Propagation of the Great Depression." *The American Economic Review* 73 (June): 257–76.

———. 1986. "Employment, Hours and Earnings in the Depression: An Analysis of Eight Manufacturing Industries." *The American Economic Review* 76 (March): 82–109.

———. 1995. "The Macroeconomics of the Great Depression: A Comparative Approach." *Journal of Money, Credit and Banking* 27 (February): 1–28.

Bernanke, Ben S., and Martin L. Parkinson. 1989. "Unemployment, Inflation, and Wages in the American Depression: Are There Lessons for Europe?" *American Economic Review* 79 (May): 210–14.

———. 1991. "Procyclical Labor Productivity and Competing Theories of the

Business Cycle: Some Evidence from Interwar U.S. Manufacturing Industries." *Journal of Political Economy* 99 (June): 439–59.

Bierman, Harold, Jr. 1991. *The Great Myths of 1929 and the Lessons to be
Learned.* New York: Greenwood Press.

Bolch, Ben, Rendigs Fels, and Marshall McMahon. 1971. "Housing Surplus in
the 1920s?" *Explorations in Economic History* 8 (spring): 259–83.

Bonnell, Sheila. 1981. "Real Wages and Employment in the Great Depression."
The Economic Record 57 (September): 277–81.

Boyer, Richard O., and Herbert M. Morais. 1970. *Labor's Untold Story.* 3d ed.
New York: United Electrical, Radio and Machine Workers of America.

Braun, Hans-Joachim. 1990. *The German Economy in the Twentieth Century.*
London: Routledge.

Brown, E. Cary. 1956. "Fiscal Policy in the 'Thirties: A Reappraisal." *The American Economic Review* 46 (December): 857–79.

Buckley, John, ed. 1989. *Guide to World Commodity Markets.* 6th ed. Chicago:
Probus Publishing.

Burbidge, J., and A. Harrison. 1985. "A Historical Decomposition of the Great
Depression to Determine the Role of Money." *Journal of Monetary Economics* 16 (July): 45–54.

Cagan, Phillip. 1956. "The Monetary Dynamics of Hyperinflation." In Milton
Friedman, ed., *Studies in the Quantity Theory of Money.* Chicago: University of Chicago Press.

Campagna, Anthony S. 1987. *U.S. National Economic Policy 1917–1985.* New
York: Praeger Publishing.

Cecchetti, Stephen G., and Georgios Karras. 1991. "Sources of Output Fluctuations During the Interwar Period: Further Evidence on the Causes of the
Great Depression." Unpublished manuscript, Ohio State University.

"Census of Partial Employment, Unemployment and Occupations." 1938. *Final
Report on Total and Partial Unemployment: United States Summary.* Washington, D.C.: U.S. Government Printing Office.

Chandler, Lester V. 1958. *Benjamin Strong, Central Banker.* Washington, D.C.:
Brookings Institution.

———. 1970. *America's Greatest Depression 1929–1941.* New York: Harper
and Row.

Cooper, Russell, and John Haltiwanger. 1993. "Automobiles and the National
Industrial Recovery Act: Evidence on Industry Complementarities." *Quarterly Journal of Economics* 103 (November): 1044–71.

Council of Economic Advisors. *Economic Report of the President.* Washington,
D.C.: U.S. Government Printing Office, various issues.

Degen, Robert A. 1987. *The American Monetary System: A Concise Survey of Its
Evolution Since 1896* Lexington, Mass.: Lexington Books.

DeLong, J. Bradford, and Lawrence H. Summers. 1986. "The Changing Cyclical
Variability of Economic Activity in the United States." In Robert J. Gordon,
ed., *The American Business Cycle: Continuity and Change.* Chicago: University of Chicago Press.

Diba, Behzad T., and Herschel I. Grossman. 1988. "Explosive Rational Bubbles
in Stock Prices?" *American Economic Review* 78 (June): 520–29.

Dornbusch, Rudiger, and Stanley Fischer. 1986. "The Open Economy: Implications for Monetary and Fiscal Policy." In Robert J. Gordon, ed., *The American Business Cycle: Continuity and Change.* Chicago: University of Chicago Press.

Eastburn, David P. 1965. *The Federal Reserve on Record.* Philadelphia: Federal Reserve Bank of Philadelphia.

Eichengreen, Barry. 1992a. "'IT' Can Happen Again." *Challenge* (November/December): 14–19.

————. 1992b. *Golden Fetters: The Gold Standard and the Great Depression, 1919–1939.* New York: Oxford University Press.

Epstein, Gerald, and Thomas Ferguson. 1984. "Monetary Policy, Loan Liquidation, and Industrial Conflict: The Federal Reserve and the Open Market Operations of 1932." *Journal of Economic History* XLIV:957–84.

Evans, Martin, and Paul Wachtel. 1993. "Were Price Changes during the Great Depression Anticipated? Evidence from Nominal Interest Rates." *Journal of Monetary Economics* 32 (August): 3–34.

Fackler, James S., and Randall E. Parker. 1994. "Accounting for the Great Depression: A Historical Decomposition." *Journal of Macroeconomics* 16 (spring): 193–220.

Faulkner, Harold Underwood. 1960. *American Economic History.* 8th ed. New York: Harper and Row.

Federal Reserve Act of 1913. HR 7837, Vol. 38, *United States Statutes at Large,* 63d Congress, 1913–1915.

Federal Reserve Board of Governors. *Federal Reserve Bulletin.* Washington, D.C.: various issues.

————. 1943. *Banking and Monetary Statistics, 1914–1941.* Washington, D.C.

Field, Alexander James. 1992. "Uncontrolled Land Development and the Duration of the Depression in the United States." *Journal of Economic History* 52 (December): 785–805.

Fisher, Irving. 1933. "The Debt-Deflation Theory of Great Depressions." *Econometrica* 1 (October): 337–57.

Flacco, Paul R., and Randall E. Parker. 1992. "Income Uncertainty and the Onset of the Great Depression." *Economic Inquiry* 30 (January): 154–71.

Flood, Mark D. 1992. "The Great Deposit Insurance Debate." Federal Reserve Bank of St. Louis *Review* 74 (July/August): 51–77.

Friedman, Milton. 1956. "The Demand for Money: Some Theoretical and Empirical Results." Reprinted in Milton Friedman, ed., *The Optimum Quantity of Money and Other Essays.* Chicago: Aldine Publishing, 1969.

————. 1970. "Comments on the Critics." In Robert J. Gordon, ed., *Milton Friedman's Monetary Framework: A Debate with His Critics.* Chicago: University of Chicago Press.

Friedman, Milton, and Anna J. Schwartz. 1963. *A Monetary History of the United States, 1867–1960.* Princeton: Princeton University Press.

————. 1982. *Monetary Trends in the United States and the United Kingdom.* Chicago: University of Chicago Press.

Galbraith, John Kenneth. 1954. *The Great Crash 1929.* Boston: Houghton Mifflin.

Garside, W. R. 1990. *British Unemployment 1919–1939.* Cambridge: Cambridge University Press.

Gordon, Robert A. 1961. *Business Fluctuations.* 2d ed. New York: Harper and Row.

Gordon, Robert J. 1980. "Postwar Macroeconomics: The Evolution of Events and Ideas." In Martin Feldstein, ed., *The American Economy in Transition.* Chicago: University of Chicago Press.

———. 1988. "Back to the Future: European Unemployment Today Viewed from America in 1939." *Brookings Papers on Economic Activity,* no. 1, 271–304.

———. 1993. *Macroeconomics.* 6th ed. New York: HarperCollins.

Gordon, Robert J., and John M. Veitch. 1986. "Fixed Investment in the American Business Cycle, 1919–1983." In Robert J. Gordon, ed., *The American Business Cycle: Continuity and Change.* Chicago: University of Chicago Press.

Gordon, Robert J., and James A. Wilcox. 1981. "Monetarist Interpretations of the Great Depression: An Evaluation and Critique." In Karl Brunner, ed., *The Great Depression Revisited.* Boston: Kluwer-Nijhoff Publishing.

Haberler, Gottfried. 1958. *Prosperity and Depression.* 4th ed. Cambridge: Cambridge University Press.

Hacker, Louis M. 1934. *A Short History of the New Deal.* New York: F. S. Crofts.

Hall, Thomas E. 1990. *Business Cycles: The Nature and Causes of Economic Fluctuations.* New York: Praeger Publishing.

Hamilton, James D. 1987. "Monetary Factors in the Great Depression." *Journal of Monetary Economics* 19:145–69.

———. 1992. "Was the Deflation During the Great Depression Anticipated? Evidence from the Commodity Futures Market." *American Economic Review* 82 (March): 157–78.

Hardach, Gerd. 1984. "Banking and Industry in Germany in the Interwar Period 1919–1939." *Journal of European Economic History* 13 (fall, special issue): 203–34.

Haubrich, Joseph G. 1990. "Nonmonetary Effects of Financial Crises: Lessons from the Great Depression in Canada." *Journal of Monetary Economics* 25 (March): 223–52.

Herzstein, Robert Edwin, and the Editors of Time-Life Books. 1980. *The Nazis.* Alexandria, Va.: Time-Life Books.

Hoover, Herbert. 1952. *The Memoirs of Herbert Hoover: The Great Depression, 1929–1941.* New York: Macmillan.

Hubbard, R. Glenn, and Peter C. Reiss. 1989. "Corporate Payouts and the Tax Price of Corporate Retentions: Evidence from the Undistributed Profits Tax of 1936–1938." National Bureau of Economic Research working paper no. 3111.

Hughes, Johnathan. 1987. *American Economic History.* 2d ed. Glenview, Ill.: Scott, Foresman and Co.

James, Harold. 1986. *The German Slump.* Oxford: Clarendon Press.

Jones, Joseph M., Jr. 1934. *Tariff Retaliation*. Philadelphia: University of Pennsylvania Press.

Kemp, Jack. 1979. *An American Renaissance*. New York: Harper and Row.

Keynes, John Maynard. 1919. "Proposals for the Reconstruction of Europe (1919)." Reprinted in J. M. Keynes, ed., *Essays in Persuasion*. New York: Norton, 1963.

———. 1925. "The Economic Consequences of Mr. Churchill (1925)." Reprinted in J. M. Keynes, ed., *Essays in Persuasion*. New York: Norton, 1963.

———. 1930. "The Great Slump of 1930 (1930)." Reprinted in J. M. Keynes, ed., *Essays in Persuasion*. New York: Norton, 1963.

———. 1931. "The End of the Gold Standard (September 27, 1931)." Reprinted in J. M. Keynes, ed., *Essays in Persuasion*. New York: Norton, 1963.

———. 1936. *The General Theory of Employment, Interest, and Money*. London: Macmillan.

Kindleberger, Charles P. 1986. *The World in Depression, 1929–1939*. Berkeley: University of California Press.

Kirby, M. W. 1981. *The Decline of British Economic Power Since 1870*. London: George Allen and Unwin.

Klein, Lawrence R. 1947. *The Keynesian Revolution*. New York: Macmillan.

Knight-Ridder Financial Publishing. 1994. *Commodity Perspectives: Encyclopedia of Historical Charts*. New York: Knight-Ridder Financial Publishing.

Kroszner, Randall S., and Raghurum G. Rajan. 1994. "Is the Glass-Steagall Act Justified? A Study of the U.S. Experience with Universal Banking Before 1933." *American Economic Review* 84 (September): 810–32.

League of Nations. 1932. *World Economic Survey 1931–32*. Geneva: League of Nations.

———. *Monthly Bulletin of Statistics*, various issues.

Leijonhufvud, Axel. 1968. *On Keynesian Economics and the Economics of Keynes*. New York: Oxford University Press.

Lewis, W. Arthur. 1949. *Economic Survey 1919–1939*. New York: Harper and Row.

Leuchtenburg, William E. 1958. *The Perils of Prosperity 1914–32*. Chicago: University of Chicago Press.

———. 1963. *Franklin Roosevelt and the New Deal*. New York: Harper and Row.

Liu, Tung, Gary J. Santoni, and Courtenay C. Stone. 1995. "In Search of Stock Market Bubbles: A Comment on Rappoport and White." *Journal of Economic History* 55 (September): 647–54.

Lucas, Robert E. 1993. "Making a Miracle." *Econometrica* 61 (March): 251–72.

Malkiel, Burton G. 1963. "Equity Yields, Growth, and the Structure of Share Prices." *American Economic Review* 53 (December): 1004–31.

Mascaro, Angelo, and Allan H. Meltzer. 1983. "Long and Short Term Interest Rates in a Risky World." *Journal of Monetary Economics* 12 (November 1983), 485–518.

McCallum, Bennett. 1990. "Could a Monetary Base Rule Have Prevented the Great Depression?" *Journal of Monetary Economics* 26 (August): 3–26.

Meltzer, Allan H. 1976. "Monetary and Other Explanations of the Great Depression." *Journal of Monetary Economics* 2:455–71.

————. 1995. "Monetary, Credit and (Other) Transmission Processes: A Monetarist Perspective." *Journal of Economic Perspectives* 9 (fall): 49–72.

Meltzer, Milton. 1969. *Brother, Can You Spare A Dime?* New York: Alfred A. Knopf.

Mishkin, Frederic S. 1978. "The Household Balance Sheet and the Great Depression." *Journal of Economic History* 38 (December): 918–37.

Moure, Kenneth. 1991. *Managing the Franc Poincare.* Cambridge: Cambridge University Press.

Nanto, Dick K., and Shinji Takagi. 1985. "Korekiyo Takahashi and Japan's Recovery from the Great Depression." *The American Economic Review* 75 (May): 369–74.

Nathan, Otto. 1944. *The Nazi Economic System.* New York: Russell and Russell.

O'Brien, Anthony. 1985. "The Cyclical Sensitivity of Wages." *The American Economic Review* 75 (December): 1124–32.

Overy, R. J. 1982. *The Nazi Economic Recovery.* London: Macmillan Press.

Owen, Robert L. 1919. *The Federal Reserve Act.* New York: The Century Company.

Patrick, Hugh. 1971. "The Economic Muddle of the 1920s." In J. W. Morley, ed., *Dilemmas of Growth in Prewar Japan.* Princeton: Princeton University Press.

Petzina, Dietmar. 1990. "Was There a Crisis Before the Crisis? The State of the German Economy in the 1920s." In Jurgen Baron Von Kruedener, ed., *Economic Crisis and Political Collapse: The Weimar Republic, 1924–1933.* New York: Berg Publishers.

Pope, Rex, and Bernard Hoyle, eds. 1985. *British Economic Performance 1880–1980.* London: Croom Helm.

Potter, Jim. 1974. *The American Economy Between the World Wars.* London: Macmillan Press.

Rappoport, Peter, and Eugene N. White. 1994. "Was the Crash of 1929 Expected?" *American Economic Review* 84 (March): 271–81.

Reading, Don. 1973. "New Deal Activity and the States, 1933 to 1939." *Journal of Economic History* 33:792–810.

Remarque, Erich Maria. 1931. *The Road Back.* Boston: Little, Brown, and Co.

Reynolds, Lloyd G., Stanley H. Masters, and Celletta H. Moser. 1991. *Labor Economics and Labor Relations.* 10th ed. Englewood Cliffs: Prentice Hall.

Richardson, H. W. 1967. *Economic Recovery in Britain 1932–1939.* London: Weidenfeld and Nicolson.

Robert, Karl. 1941. *Hitler's Counterfeit Reich.* New York: Alliance Book Corp.

Roberts, Stephen H. 1937. *The House That Hitler Built.* New York: Harper and Brothers.

Rolfe, Sidney E., and James Burtle. 1973. *The Great Wheel: The World Monetary System.* New York: Quadrangle/New York Times Book Co.

Romer, Christina D. 1990. "The Great Crash and the Onset of the Great Depression." *The Quarterly Journal of Economics* 105 (August): 597–624.

————. 1992. "What Ended the Great Depression?" *Journal of Economic History* 52 (December): 757–84.

————. 1993. "The Nation in Depression." *Journal of Economic Perspectives* 7 (spring): 19–39.

Sadler, A. L. 1946. *A Short History of Japan.* Sydney: Angus and Robertson.

Samuelson, Paul A. 1948. *Economics: An Introductory Analysis.* New York: McGraw Hill.

Santoni, Gary J. 1987. "The Great Bull Markets of 1924–29 and 1982–87: Speculative Bubbles or Economic Fundamentals?" Federal Reserve Bank of St. Louis *Review* 69 (November): 16–29.

Sargent, Thomas J. 1986. *Rational Expectations and Inflation.* New York: Harper and Row.

Schwartz, Anna J. 1981. "Understanding 1929–1933." In Karl Brunner, ed., *The Great Depression Revisited.* Boston: Kluwer-Nijhoff Publishing.

Shiller, Robert J. 1981. "Do Stock Prices Move Too Much to be Justified by Subsequent Changes in Dividends?" *American Economic Review* 71 (June): 421–36.

Shirer, William L. 1960. *The Rise and Fall of the Third Reich: A History of Nazi Germany.* New York: Simon and Schuster.

Sirkin, Gerald. 1975. "The Stock Market of 1929 Revisited: A Note." *Business History Review* 49 (summer): 223–31.

Sohn-Rethel, Alfred. 1978. *Economy and Class Structure of German Fascism.* London: CSE Books.

Sommariva, Andrea, and Giuseppe Tullio. 1987. *German Macroeconomic History, 1880–1979.* New York: St. Martin's Press.

Soule, George. 1947. *The Prosperity Decade: From War to Depression, 1917–1929.* New York: Holt Rinehart.

Stolper, Gustav. 1940. *German Economy 1870–1940.* New York: Reynal and Hitchock.

Stricker, Frank. 1983–84. "Causes of the Great Depression, or What Reagan Doesn't Know About the 1920s." *Economic Forum* 14 (winter): 41–58.

Temin, Peter. 1976. *Did Monetary Forces Cause the Great Depression?* New York: W. W. Norton and Company.

————. 1989. *Lessons from the Great Depression.* Cambridge: MIT Press.

Tobin, James, and William C. Brainard. 1968. "Pitfalls in Financial Model Building." *American Economic Review Papers and Proceedings* 58 (May): 99–122.

Toland, John. 1976. *Adolf Hitler.* New York: Ballantine Books.

U.S. Department of Commerce. 1966. *Long Term Economic Growth 1860–1965.* Washington, D.C.: U.S. Government Printing Office.

Vedder, Richard K., and Lowell E. Gallaway. 1993. *Out of Work: Unemployment and Government in Twentieth-Century America.* New York: Holmes and Mayer Publishers.

Vincent, C. Paul. 1985. *The Politics of Hunger: The Allied Blockade of Germany, 1915–1919.* Athens: Ohio University Press.

Weintraub, Stanley. 1985. *A Stillness Heard Round The World.* Oxford: Oxford University Press.

Weinstein, Michael M. 1980. *Recovery and Redistribution under the NIRA.* Amsterdam: North-Holland.

Williamson, Harold F., ed. 1951. *The Growth of the American Economy.* 2d ed. Englewood Cliffs: Prentice Hall.

Williamson, Jeffrey G., and Peter H. Lindert. 1980. *American Inequality: A Macroeconomic History.* New York: Academic Press.

Wright, Gavin. 1974. "The Political Economy of New Deal Spending: An Econometric Analysis." *Review of Economics and Statistics* 56:30–38.

Index